Instant ACID®

Instant ACID®

John Rofrano and Iacobus

San Francisco, CA

Published by CMP Books
an imprint of CMP Media LLC
600 Harrison Street, 6th Floor, San Francisco, CA 94107 USA
Tel: 415-947-6615; Fax: 415-947-6015
www.cmpbooks.com
email: books@cmp.com

Distributed in the U.S. by:
Publishers Group West
1700 Fourth Street
Berkeley, CA 94710
1-800-788-3123

Distributed in Canada by:
Jaguar Book Group
100 Armstrong Avenue
Georgetown, Ontario M6K 3E7 Canada
905-877-4483

For individual orders and for information on special discounts for quantity orders, please contact:
CMP Books Distribution Center, 6600 Silacci Way, Gilroy, CA 95020
email: cmp@rushorder.com; Web: www.cmpbooks.com

ISBN: 1-57820-266-3

Dedication

To my wife Terry and my three children Johnny Jr., Michael, and Chrissy; you are my inspiration and my life. To my Father, I wish you could be here to see it. I finally did it Dad. —John Rofrano

To my Dad, my Mom, my Nana, my brother and especially my sister. To my various aunts and uncles way too numerous to list here as well as the rest of my very big family. (You know who you are.) To the United States armed forces around the world that protect the freedoms all of us enjoy (and some take for granted). God bless America. Let freedom ring. —Iacobus

From The Authors,

We have tried to fill this book with enough basics to get you productive quickly and enough tips and techniques to keep you exploring new directions. Obviously all of the functions cannot be covered in an Instant book, but we covered the ones that we use most often and hopefully they will provide you with a reference for your work with ACID. We hope you get as much out of reading it as we did writing it. If you have any questions, you can always find us on the Sony ACID Forums http://mediasoftware. sonypictures.com/forums/ (John Rofrano is JohnnyRoy and Iacobus is mD)

Foreword

The release of this book, *Instant ACID*°, marks an important milestone for the Instant book series. Not only is it the first Instant Series release of 2005, it also completes the circle of Instant books for the core Sony Media Software products. We are proud to partner with CMP as the first entity to publish training books for all three programs, Vegas°, Sound Forge°, and ACID°.

Johnny Rofrano and Iacobus, both beta testers and ACID enthusiasts from the early days of the software, remain visible as contributors to online forums and ACID communities. It is their intimacy with the program and the user communities that has allowed them to identify the most important aspects of the software for musicians and non-musicians alike. Their approach to the software and the style of the Instant books make this a must-read for any ACID enthusiast, no matter the level. We're sure you'll learn a lot from the book. But more importantly, you'll learn to have fun making music in ACID.
Enjoy!

Mannie Frances
Managing Director, VASST, Sundance Media Group

Contents

Chapter 1

Introduction

ACID is a highly graphical program that can be used on many levels. Beginners and non-musicians can use it for basic loop-based composition, drawing on the enormous talent of the loop creators, and assemble a song simply by painting loops on the Timeline. Musicians can augment existing loops by recoding their own loops, or by using ACID, as you would any recording software to create entire tracks that don't loop.

Since the introduction of ACID Pro 4, ACID can be used to record MIDI tracks and MIDI loops using outboard MIDI synthesizers or the onboard Virtual Studio Technology (VST) instruments. These features provide you with an entire recording studio right in your computer.

Track Area

The track area is where you will be doing most of your work. As you drop loops into this area from the Explorer view, new tracks will appear. Unlike other audio recording software that you might be familiar with, ACID can have only one audio loop or MIDI file on each track. You cannot combine different loops on a track. Because of this, your project track count will grow rapidly.

ACID Pro 5.0 has a new feature called Folder tracks to address this rapid expansion of tracks. Folder tracks allow you to group tracks together into folders and collapse those folders, freeing up valuable screen space. You can still work with events in the collapsed folder track, or you can open the folder track and work on them at full height.

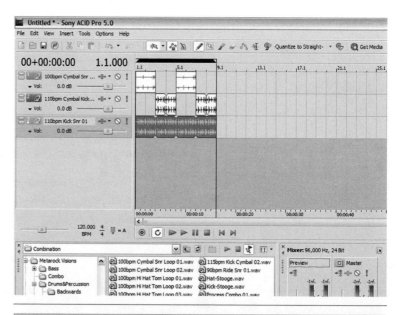

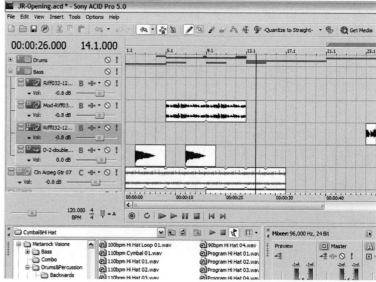

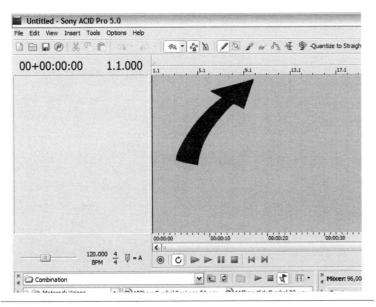

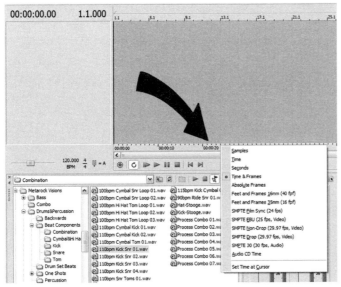

Beat Rulers and Time Rulers

The Beat Ruler is at the top of the track area. This gives you a reference for placing loops in musical time—beats and measures.

As you can see in the illustration, the measures are numbered 1.1, 2.1, 3.1, etc. The first number is the measure followed by a period, and a second number is the beat. If you zoom in on the track using the mouse wheel or up and down arrow keys, you will see finer measurements such as 2.1, 2.3, 2.3, meaning measure 2 beat 1, measure 2 beat 2, etc. You will most often use the Beat Ruler to draw your loops so that they start and end on measure or beat boundaries.

The Time Ruler is at the bottom of the track area and is off by default. To turn the Time Ruler on:

• Select View>Time Ruler>Show Time Ruler

The Time Ruler shows the wall-clock time of the song. As you change the tempo, the beat ruler will stay the same, but the Time Ruler will expand or shrink to show the change in time. You can change the format of the Time Ruler display by right-clicking on it and selecting a new format from the Context menu.

Multiple Docking Areas

At the bottom of the ACID interface is the default docking area. The left side of this area contains the Explorer window, which allows you to browse your hard drive to find and preview loops for your composition. You can compose music by simply dragging loops from the Explorer window into the Track window and painting them on the new track.

The Media Manager is a relational database that allows you to quickly and easily search all the media in your loop library by attributes of the media. Once set up, this saves hours of searching for the right loop in the directories of your hard drive.

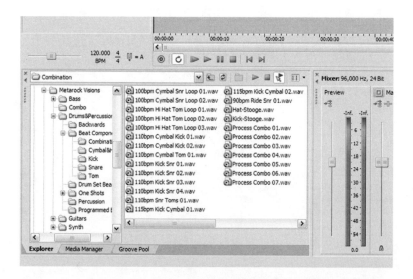

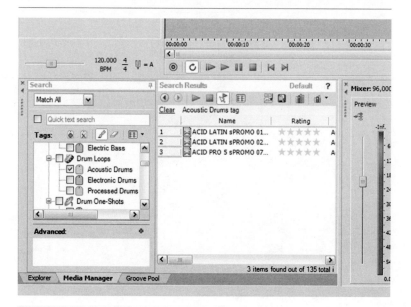

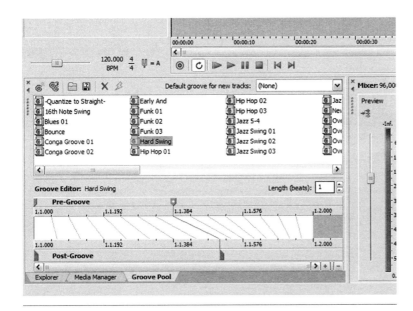

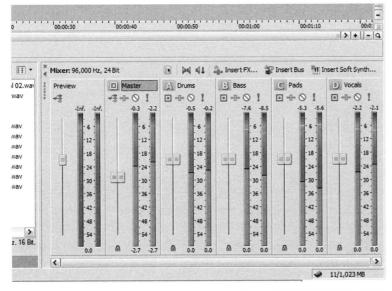

The Groove Pool stores all of your grooves. ACID Pro 5.0 ships with 51 grooves that you can apply to your loops to change their timing. You can also make your own grooves and store them in the pool. Grooves modify the loop playback, allowing you, for example, to take a straight beat and turn it into a swing beat if that's what your music calls for.

On the right ride of the docking area are all of the buses, including the Master bus, Audio buses, FX buses, and Soft Synth buses. New in ACID Pro 5.0 is Multiport VST instruments support. This means that Soft Synths that have multiple outputs have a bus for every stereo output. There is also an optional video preview window for previewing your movie when you are scoring for video. The video preview can be turned on and off using the Alt+4 key sequence or by selecting Video>Video Preview from the menu.

You can dock any of the windows from the View menu in the docking area. You can float docking areas by tearing off a docked window to float it, then drop multiple floating windows on top of each other. They will instantly form a new floating docking area that can be moved anywhere on the screen, even to a second monitor.

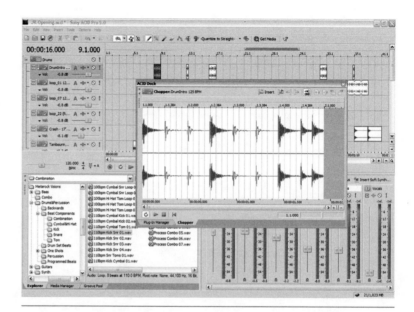

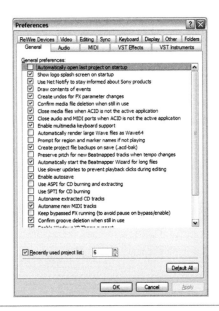

Setting Up ACID the Way YOU Work

The first thing you should do with a fresh installation of ACID is customize the interface to your preferences. A few things you should pay particular attention to so you can change them in the future if you need to are:

- *Use Net Notify to stay informed about Sony products*: This is used to check if there are updates to the ACID software. I like to leave it on.

- *Close media files when ACID is not the active application*: This is important because it allows you to edit files outside of ACID while they are still loaded into your project.

- *Close audio and MIDI ports when ACID is not the active application*: This option also affects how ACID and other applications interact. Having this checked means that ACID will give up control of audio and MIDI ports when you switch to another application, allowing that application to use the ports.

ACID Pro 5.0 has quite a few options to control what directories it pulls media from. To control where these folders point:

• Select Options>Preferences>Folders

From this dialog you can not only control the default project folder but also specify different folders for Recording, Render to new, Chop to new, New MIDI files, Extract from CD, and the Render project folder. If your needs are not that elaborate, you can keep everything for one project in the same folder. This is the "Use a single default folder for project media saves" option. In addition, the drop-down list has a special value called Project. This defaults all media saves to your current project folder. If you start all new projects in a new folder, this will keep all your media together.

The other option to watch is the "Temporary files folder." If you have a temporary directory on your PC that you like all of your temporary files to be placed in, this is where you set it. This way you need only one place to clean up temporary disk space.

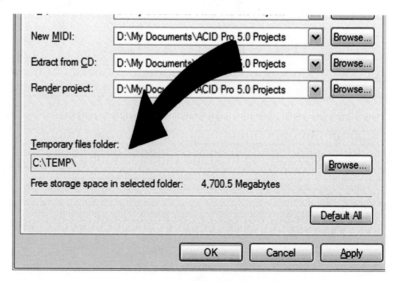

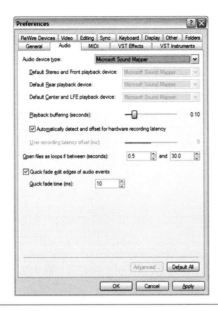

Another preference you will want to set is your audio device.

1. Click the Audio tab.

2. Pick your sound card from the "Audio device type" drop-down list.

3. Press the Apply button.

If you have a low-latency, ASIO-capable audio device, you'll want to select it here and configure it using Advanced button. The Advanced button will be available only after you click Apply.

If you get an error that your ASIO device doesn't support the current sample rate or bit depth, you will need to change your project settings to conform to a sample rate and bit depth supported by your soundcard.

To Change the default project settings:

1. Select File>Properties or press Alt+Enter.

2. Click the Audio tab.

3. Change the Sample rate (Hz) and bit depth to match your soundcard specifications.

4. Check "Start all new projects with these settings."

5. Click OK.

All of your new projects will start with the sample rate and bit depth you have selected.

Chapter 2

Fundamentals of Looping

Looping is what ACID is all about. In 1998 ACID took the industry by storm when it first introduced the concept of building music from loops. Loops are small—just a few bars of instruments recorded so that they loop seamlessly from measure to measure. After all, most music is a collection of re-petitive themes. Many pop songs can be dissected into intro, verse, chorus, bridge, and ending with variations on the number of times a verse repeats before a chorus or the number of verse and chorus combinations before a bridge. The key word is "repeats."

Loops are very helpful for a solo composer. I often browse through my loop libraries looking for inspiration. I'll find a drum beat that strikes me, and I'll start jamming with it on keyboard. Before you know it, a song is born.

ACID Properties/ACIDization

ACID maintains properties in the metadata of a wave file that tell it how to
interpret that wave when it is brought
into ACID. The process of adding this
metadata is known as ACIDization or
to ACIDize. Many audio programs will
also read this data and treat the loops
appropriately. If a wave file is not
ACIDized, there is no way for ACID to
know how to interpret it with regard to
tempo and stretching.

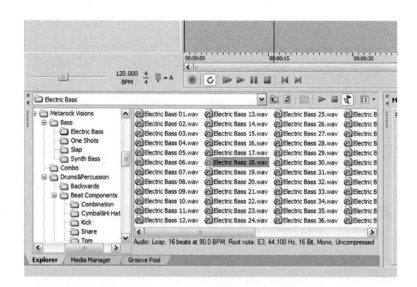

Loops, Beatmapped Tracks, and One Shots

ACIDized files can be loops, beatmapped tracks, or one-shots.

- **Loops:** wave files that are usually
  only one or two measures in length,
  although the metadata allows for
  up to 41 measures. The properties
  maintained for loops are the root
  note for transposing, and the number of beats for time stretching.
  There is a special value for the root
  note called "Don't transpose." This
  is used for loops that should not
  respond to key changes like drum
  loops.

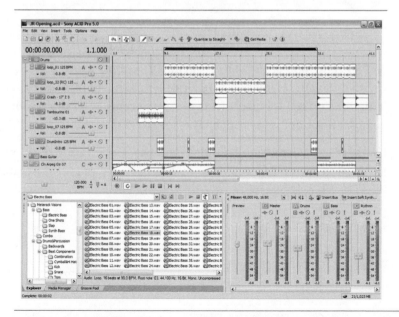

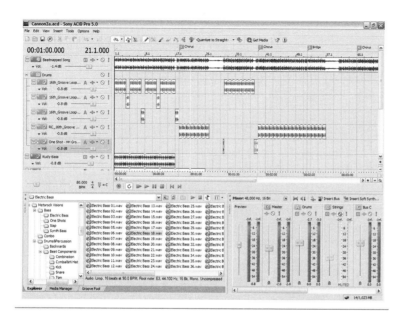

- **Beatmapped tracks:** files more than 30 seconds in length. These are usually entire songs that have been tempo-mapped. The properties maintained for beatmapped tracks are the root note for transposing, the tempo in beats per measure, and the offset of the first downbeat. Beatmapped tracks also have a "Don't transpose" value for their root note. This is used when beatmapping songs that you may want to make slower or faster but don't want to change key.

- **One-shot:** a wave file that does not loop and has no concept of tempo. This is used for hits like cymbal crashes, single drumbeats, or instrument sounds. They play for their duration and then stop.

All of the compositions that you create in ACID will be built from a combination of these three building blocks.

Each of these loop types resides in a track of the same type. In addition to these fundamental types of tracks, there are two more track types:

- **MIDI tracks:** tracks with MIDI files instead of audio files. They behave like loop tracks in that the events repeat when sized beyond their end. They also respond to tempo data. If you set their root key to something other than "don't transpose" they with respond to key change data, too.

- **Folder tracks:** new for ACID Pro 5.0, containers for other tracks, including other folder tracks. They provide a hierarchical grouping mechanism for organizing tracks.

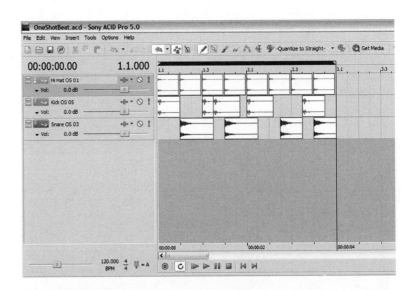

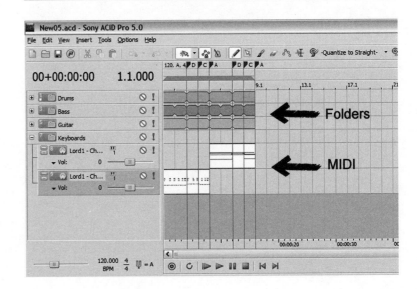

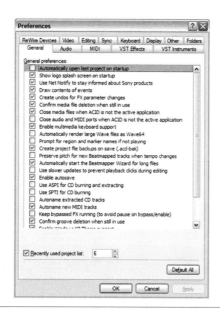

Our First Project

ACID will load the last project you were working on. If, however, you usually work on different projects every time you start ACID, then it may be a waste of time to wait for the last project to load, especially if it contains many tracks of VST instruments. You can change this behavior.

To have ACID not load the last project on startup:

1. Select Options>Preferences.

2. The General tab should be showing. If it isn't, click on it.

3. Check or uncheck the first option, "Automatically open last project on startup."

To start a new project:

*   Select File>New or click the New icon on the toolbar.

Drag, Drop, and Paint

One of the biggest errors beginning users make is that they forget the paint part. ACID won't make any sounds unless you paint the loops on the tracks.

Start by selecting the Explorer Window tab at the bottom of the docking area. From the Explorer you can navigate the files and folders on your hard drive. When you click on a wave file it will play so that you can audition it. The bottom of the file display will show you the following information about the file:

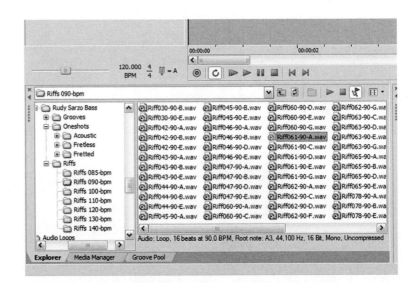

- The type of ACID wave file

- How many beats it contains

- How many beats per measure

- Root note (if any)

- Sample frequency

- Sample bit depth

This information is useful, because although ACID can time stretch your loops to match the tempo of your song, too much time stretching will result in unwanted artifacts during playback.

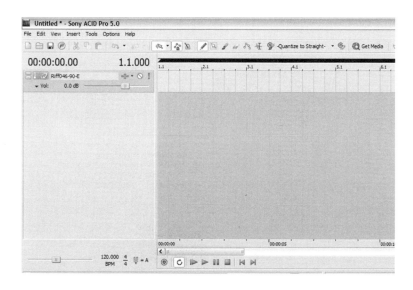

1. Drag a file and drop it on the Timeline.

A new empty track will appear for this loop. If you click the Play from Start (Shift+F12) button, nothing will play. Why? Because ACID has loaded the loop into an empty track but it doesn't know where you want to play the loop. You must paint events on the track to tell ACID when to play the loop.

You can replace the loop in a track by dragging a new loop to the track header and dropping it.

2. Select the Draw Tool (Ctrl+D) if it isn't already selected. It's the one that looks like a pencil.

3. Drag the Draw Tool across the track you just created to paint events on it.

ACID will draw the loop for as long as you continue dragging. This is how you tell ACID where to play the loop in relation to the Timeline. Now if you place the Timeline cursor at the beginning of the loop event and press the Play button, you will hear the loop play in the tempo and key of the project.

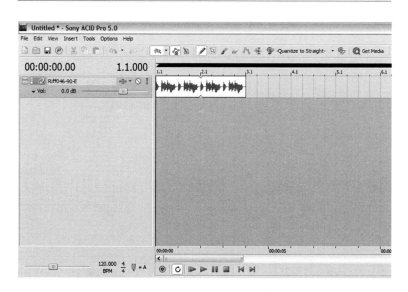

You can draw events anywhere on the Timeline with spaces between them. This allows you to control exactly when a loop will play.

4. Drop a second loop onto the Timeline.

Try to select one that is a different number of beats, or BPM, or key (root note). Use the data display at the bottom of the Explorer window to determine this.

5. Use the Draw Tool again to paint events onto the Timeline.

6. Click Play or press the spacebar.

You should hear the two loops play in sync and in the same key even though their BPM and root notes may have been different. ACID will adjust loops to play together so that you don't have to worry about these things. This is why the properties in the ACIDized loops are so important.

To play the project from the current cursor position, use the spacebar. Press the spacebar again to stop it. You can control whether the spacebar starts and stops or starts and pauses (retaining its place in the song) in the General Preferences tab.

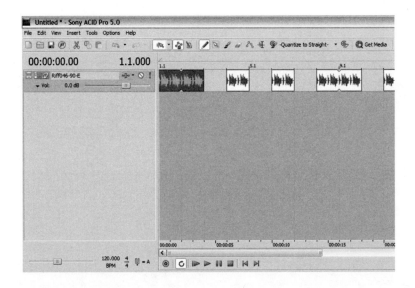

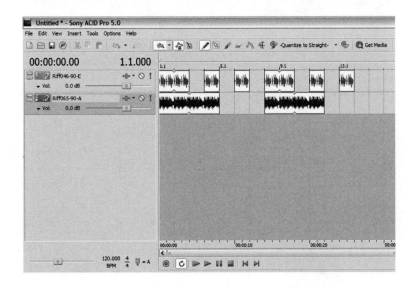

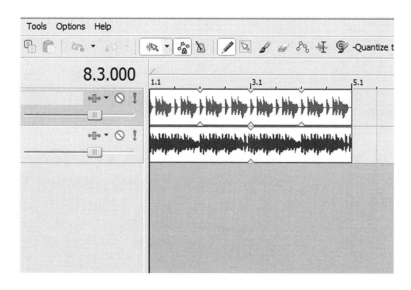

Notice that there is a little divot that displays at regular intervals in the event. These are the places where the wave file is looping. If you selected two loops that contained a different number of beats as we did in the example, the divots will display at different intervals. The top track has a loop length of four beats while the bottom track has a loop length of eight beats.

To quickly paint a loop, beatmapped, or one-shot file on the Timeline for its full duration, click the Paint Tool while pressing the Shift key.

You can also paint loops on the Timeline with the Paint Tool. It looks like a paintbrush. You don't have to drag the Paint Tool to place events on the Timeline. Just a left-click of the mouse will do. Unlike the Draw Tool, the Paint Tool works on multiple tracks without lifting the mouse. You can quickly paint a vertical set of events using the Paint Tool.

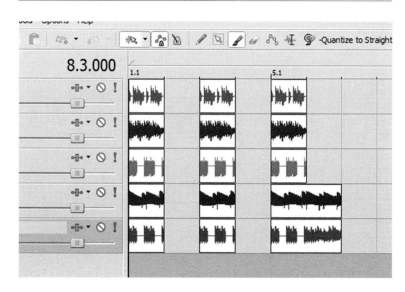

You don't have to be too concerned about painting an event beyond the point you want it to end. You can always adjust the event size after it has been drawn or painted by using the Draw Tool and hovering over either end of the event. The arrow cursor will turn into the resize cursor, and clicking and holding the left mouse button will allow you to adjust the length of the event.

The Erase Tool will also remove parts of an event equal to the current grid increment.

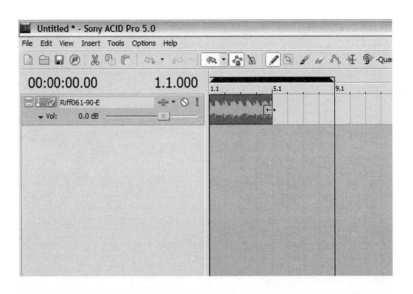

Cut, Copy, Paste, and Ripple

In addition to painting events, you can cut (Ctrl+X), copy (Ctrl+C), and paste (Ctrl+V) them as you do words in a word processor. Select the events you want to cut or copy and then move the cursor to where you want to paste them.

ACID also has ripple edits (Ctrl+L). While the cut operation leaves a whole in the track where the event was, ripple editing will fill in the space left by the event, moving everything to the left to fill it in.

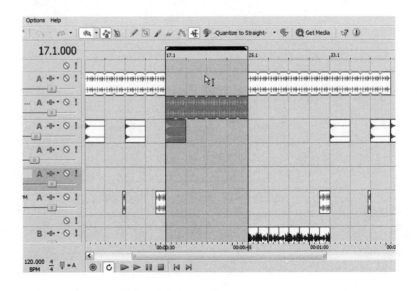

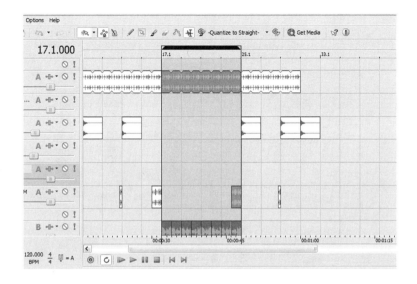

To ripple edit:

1. Turn Ripple Edit on using either Options>Ripple Edits or Ctrl+L.

2. Use the Time Selection Tool to make a selection on the Timeline that represents the area you want to cut. (Note: Ripple edit works only with the selection made by the Time Selection Tool. Do not confuse this with the regular Selection Tool. The Time Selection Tool is an icon of a wave with an 'I' cursor on top of it.)

3. Use cut (Ctrl+X) to remove the area. The space from the cut will be filled with the events from the right of it.

If you don't want to ripple all the events on the Timeline, you can select only those events you want to ripple before you make your Timeline selection. This allows you to ripple only one track, several tracks, or all tracks.

Ripple editing can also be used with paste. When you normally paste an event into the Timeline, it overlays whatever is there, and no other events move. If you paste with ripple editing turned on, all the events move to the right to make room for the new event.

Pasting with ripple edit turned on is a great way to add another verse or chorus in the middle of song.

Another great time saver is Paste Repeat. This allows you to quickly build repeating loops or one shots. If you want to lay down a 16th note hi-hat for a whole measure, Paste Repeat is the quickest way to do it.

If you find yourself turning ripple edit on and off a lot, consider adding it to the toolbar so that it is easily accessible.

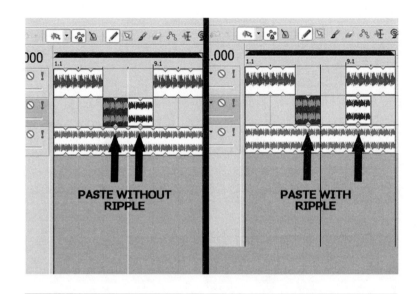

PASTE WITHOUT RIPPLE

PASTE WITH RIPPLE

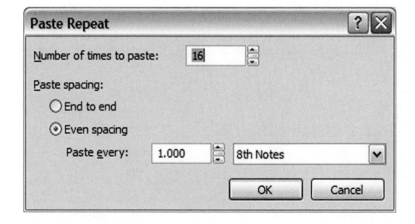

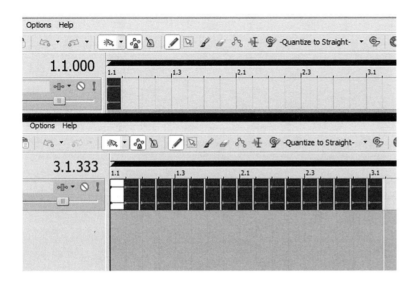

To use paste repeat:

1. Cut (Ctrl+X) or copy (Ctrl+C) the event you want to paste repeat.

2. Select Edit>Paste Repeat or press Ctrl+B.

3. In the Paste Repeat dialog box, enter the number of times to paste. For example, for a 16th note hi-hat, enter 16.

4. Select either End-to-End (which will paste the events one after the other) or Even Spacing and specify the interval and note duration. Try an interval of 1 and 16th notes to get one measure of 16th notes.

5. Click OK.

You should see the events pasted the number of times you specified. If you selected even spacing, then the events will be spaced at even intervals. For example, if you selected an interval of 1 and 16th notes, the event will be inserted every 16th note. If, however, you selected 2 and 16th notes, the event will be pasted every second 16th note. This is the same as specifying 1 and 8th notes, since every other 16th note would be on 8th note boundaries.

Changing Tempo, Time Signatures, and Keys

You can set up the initial tempo, key, and time signature by selecting the respective interface controls as shown at right. It's a good idea to do this for each project, otherwise ACID will default all your projects to 120bpm, 4/4 time in the key of A.

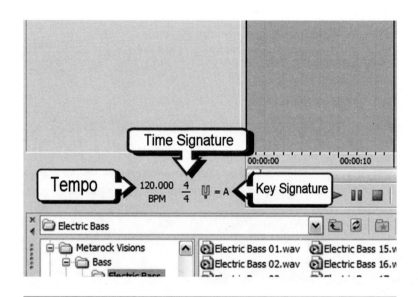

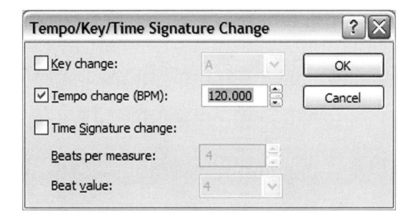

You can also change the tempo, key, and time signature during the song by adding a Tempo/Key/Time Signature Change marker.

To change the tempo, key, or time signature of a song:

1. Place the cursor at the point on the Timeline where you want the change to take place.

2. Press the T key to change the tempo, K to change the key, or Shift+K to change the time signature.

3. Type the new values into the Tempo/Key/Time Signature Change dialog box. (Note: You can change them all at the same time by enabling all three features.)

4. Click OK.

When you play your song, the change you selected will happen when playback cursor reaches that marker. A tempo change will either speed up or slow down a song, a key change will time-stretch all events that have a root key defined, and a time signature change will adjust the Time Ruler divisions and grid spacing on the Timeline as well as the downbeat of the metronome.

If you want a song to change tempo gradually, place several tempo markers at regular intervals with each one having a BPM value closer to the desired tempo.

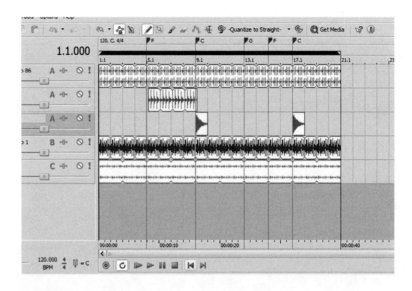

Markers, Regions, and Commands

There are several ways to annotate the parts of a song.

- **Markers** (also referred to as beat markers) are a great way of annotating a song. They stay fixed to the measure and beat in which they are placed. Markers allow you to easily navigate to them by pressing their associated number. A marker is just a particular point in time with no duration. It is useful for marking where guitar solos start or other areas you might want to get to quickly when working on a song.

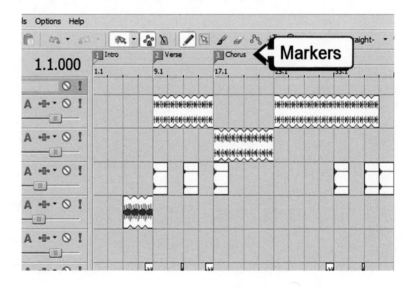

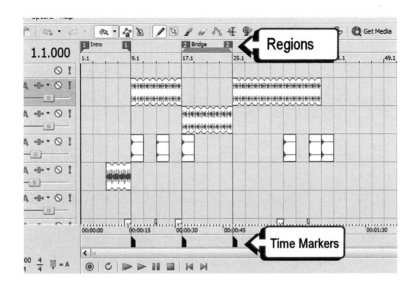

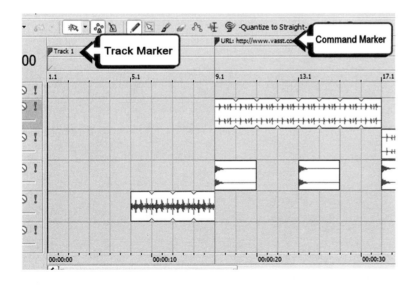

- **Time markers** are just like markers except that they stay fixed in absolute time. If you place a time marker at 1 minute and 5 seconds, no matter how you change the tempo of the song, that marker will remain fixed at 1 minute and 5 seconds. These are very useful for scoring video and are covered in Chapter 3, Considerations for Non-Linear Editors.

- **Regions** allow you to specify position and duration. They have a beginning and an end. Regions are most commonly used for annotating the sections of a song like verse, chorus, bridge, etc. You can quickly select the region by double-clicking on the top of the Timeline within the region.

- **Commands** allow you to imbed information in streaming media files. This can display titles or credits while the file is playing or invoke a URL.

- **CD track markers** (new for ACID 5) are used to delineate CD tracks when burning disk-at-once CDs. They are covered in Chapter 16, Burning the Final Project.

To add a marker:

1. Position your cursor on the Time-
    line where you want the marker to
    be.

2. Press the M key.

You can drop markers on the Timeline
while the project is playing. This is
useful for marking areas that you want
to go back to later.

To add a region:

1. Make a selection on the Timeline
    where you want the region to cover.

2. Press the R key.

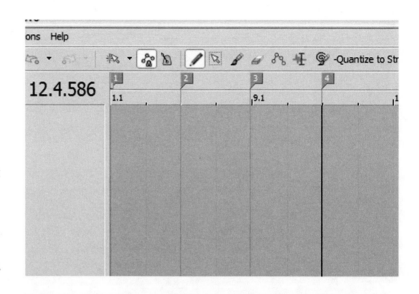

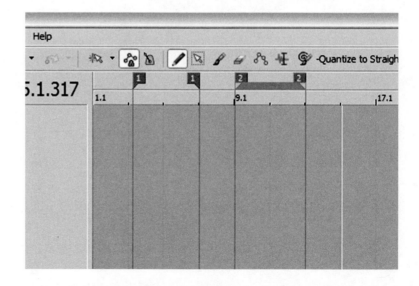

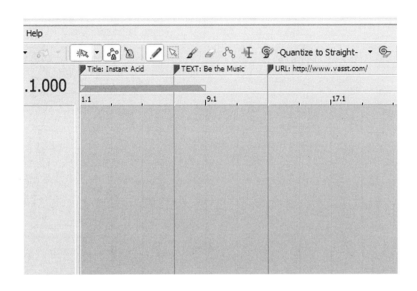

To add a command:

1. Position your cursor on the Time-line where you want the command to be.

2. Press the C key.

3. Fill in the details about the command.

4. Click OK.

You can fit a song to a particular duration using Adjust Tempo to match marker to cursor (covered in Chapter 3).

Commands can display text about the media, invoke URLs when the media finishes playing, and other various events. Check the ACID online help for all the various command options.

Saving a Project with All Its Loops

When you have finished your work session, you will want to save your project. It might be a good idea to also save all the loops associated with your project in one place. This will eliminate any errors caused by missing loops due to loops being moved on your hard drive or from using a temporary drive storage device as your loop source.

To save a project with all its media:

1. Select File>Save As.

2. Navigate to the directory where you want to save your project and specify the file name to save it under.

3. Check the box labeled "Copy all media with project."

4. Click OK.

If you need to move a project between workstations, use the "Save as type: ACID Project With Embedded Media (*.acd-zip)." This will zip all of your files into one file with the extension .acd-zip. Now you only need to copy this one file to your other workstation. ACID will load the project and the media from this single file.

Chapter 3

Considerations for Nonlinear Video Editors

ACID is an outstanding tool for nonlinear editors who need to write soundtracks for video. There are hundreds of loop libraries available that cater to almost every musical style. Whether you're looking for a upbeat pop feel or an orchestral score, there are loops available that will allow you to quickly establish a mood with just a few drag-and-drops. ACID also has tools to lock the tempo to markers for syncing music events with video events.

Working with a Video Track

ACID has the ability to work with video so that you can easily score music. It has one video track that can hold a single video file. This should be either a rough cut or final cut rendered from your nonlinear editor application (NLE). This video track is always pinned to the top of the Timeline. You cannot move it, but you can resize it vertically. As you scroll down the track list, the video track will always be visible so that you can reference it.

The first thing you will want to do when working with video is to turn the video preview window on by selecting View>Video Preview or pressing Alt+4.

The video preview will show up in the lower-right docking area. You can resize it, tear it off and have it float, or move it to a secondary display if you have one.

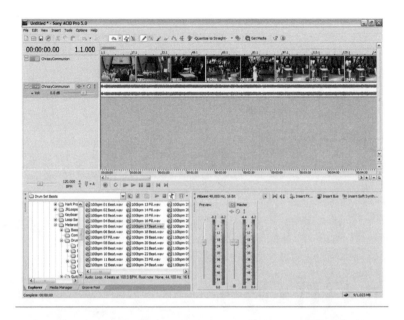

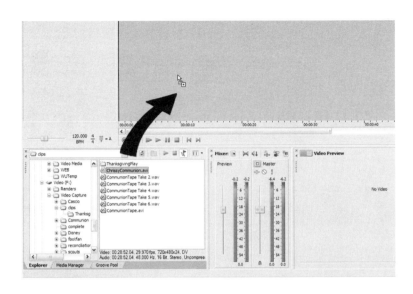

To add a video to ACID:

- Select File>Open and select your video file, or drag and drop it from Windows Explorer.

You may have only one video file in ACID at a time.

By default, the video track will show frame numbers in the video. You can change this in the preferences.

To modify the video frame numbers on thumbnails:

1. Select Options>Preferences.

2. Click on the Video tab.

3. Change the option "Show source frame numbers on event thumbnails as:" to the desired readout.

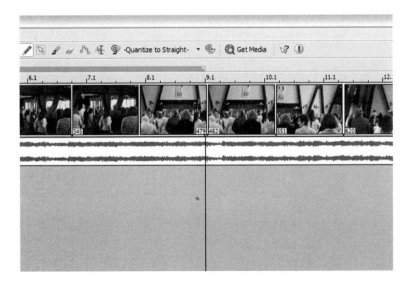

You can select from None, Frame Numbers, Time Ruler Format, Media Format. The Time Ruler Format will display the absolute hours, minutes, and seconds just like the Time Ruler does. The Media Format will display the actual time format in the media as hours, minutes, seconds, and frames. If you have cues that need to be frame-accurate, you will want to set this to Media Format.

The audio will be added as a one-shot so that ACID will not time-stretch it in any way. You want to keep it this way so the audio doesn't get out of sync with the video. You can remove the audio by deleting the track, or you can just mute the audio track so you can refer to it later. By muting the track instead of deleting it you can still see the wave form, which may give you audio cues as to when someone starts talking or other audio events that may be significant to the score.

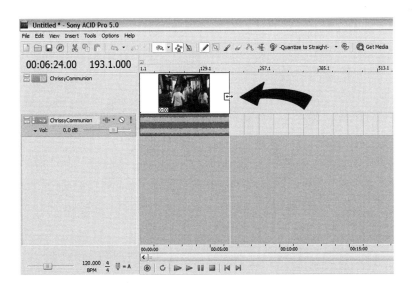

The video track may be shortened or moved just like any other ACID event, but it cannot be split or altered in any other way.

Time Markers

Time markers are tied to absolute wall-clock time. Unlike beat markers, they are affected by tempo and always represent the true time that has transpired since the beginning of the project. This is critical for scoring video because your video is running at a constant, real-time rate. When marking events in the video that you want to score always use time markers.

Double-clicking the lower scroll bar will quickly resize the Timeline to view the whole project.

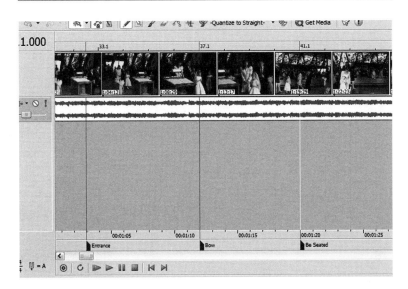

To insert a time marker:

- Select Insert>Time Marker or press the H key.

Notice that the time marker is placed at the bottom of the Timeline where the Time Ruler is. If there isn't a Time Ruler at the bottom of your Timeline you can add it with:

- View>Time Ruler>Show Time Ruler

The Time Ruler is very helpful in scoring video because it always displays absolute wall-clock time.

Time markers can be labeled just like any other marker. To label a time marker:

1. Right-click on the time marker.

2. Select Rename from the Context menu.

By labeling time markers you easily annotate when events should occur in your soundtrack.

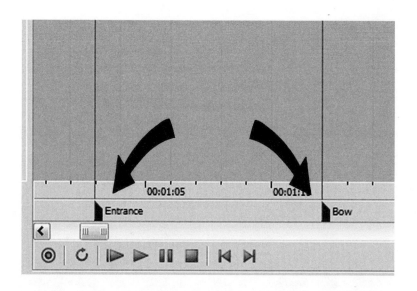

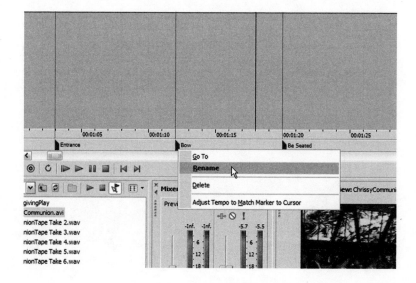

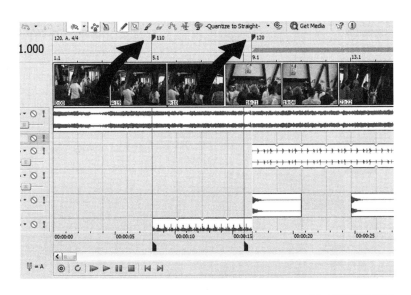

Tempo Markers

The use of tempo markers is covered in Chapter 2, Fundamentals of Looping. What is important for non-linear editors to realize is that a tempo change is not going to affect the video. The video will play at a constant speed regardless of how the tempo changes. It is the mood of the video that you should be scoring for. If there is a chase scene the music should probably be faster than in a quiet moment. By keeping the video playback consistent, ACID allows you to speed up or slow down the music without having to worry about affecting the video.

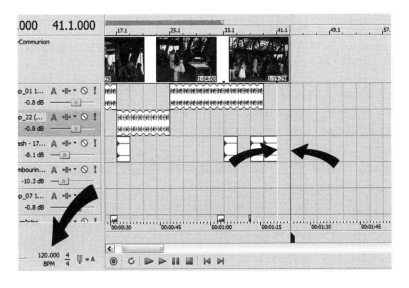

Adjusting Tempo to Match Marker to Cursor

ACID has an incredible time saver for getting a musical event to match the exact moment of a video event. It's called Adjust Tempo to Match Marker to Cursor. When you place a marker where you want a musical event to happen, then place the cursor on the actual musical event, ACID will adjust the tempo so that the event happens right on the marker.

One use of this function is to tempo-map the music to end exactly when the video ends. Before starting this example, note the tempo of the project, because it will change after these steps.

To adjust the tempo to match marker to cursor:

1. Use the H key to place a time Marker at the place in the video where you want the event to occur. (Note: This works with beat markers, too.) For this example, we will select the end of the video clip.

2. Place the cursor on the audio event that must happen at the marker. For this example, we will place the cursor at the end of the music.

3. Right-click on the Marker tab and select Adjust Tempo to Match Marker to Cursor.

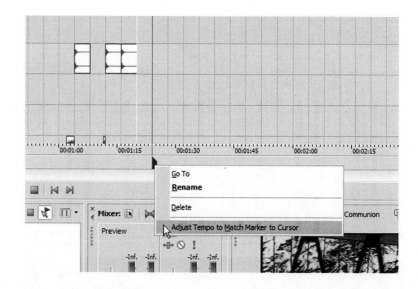

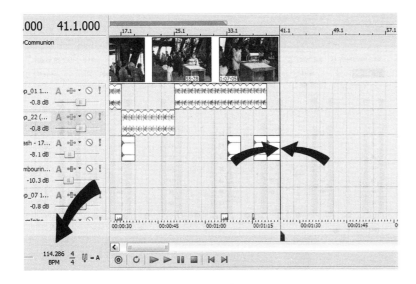

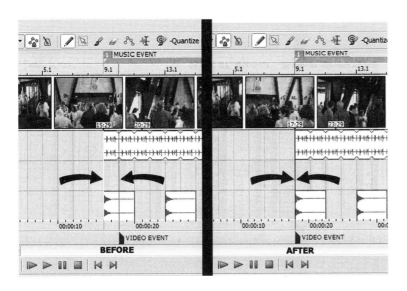

If it worked, you should see the Timeline stretch so that the end of the song is now on the marker at the end of the video. Notice that the tempo of the project has changed to compensate. The tempo change will be calculated from the last tempo marker. If there are no tempo markers in the project, the whole project tempo will change. If there are tempo markers, only the last marker to the immediate left of the cursor will be adjusted.

This could have been any point in the movie where a particular music event needed to be. Let's say you wanted the guitar solo in a song to start just as a skydiver jumps from a plane. Place a time marker at the point the person jumps, place the cursor at the beginning of the guitar solo, right-click on the Time Marker tab, and select Adjust Tempo to Match Marker to Cursor. The project tempo will be adjusted so the guitar solo starts just as the jump occurs.

Chapter 4

Tips and Tricks

Some users have their "secret weapons" when using ACID. Actually, there's really nothing secret about any of these techniques. They can be found just by playing around with ACID or if you're creative enough to come up with your own ideas. The more you know, the more creative you can become.

Reverse Parts of Your Loops

Instead of taking loops and other media at face value, use ACID 5's reverse event feature to create interest in an otherwise plain loop.

1. Select an event on the Timeline.

2. Split the event by pressing S on your keyboard.

3. Split the resulting event you just made from the last split.

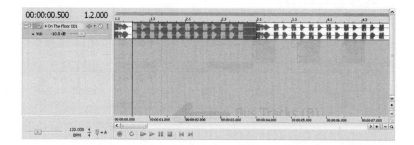

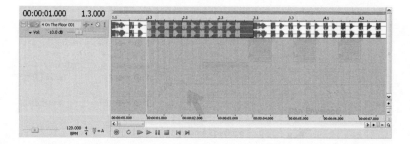

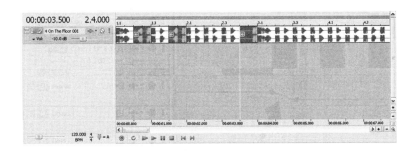

4. Repeat for as many events you want to reverse.

5. Select the events, then press U.

Use the Bus Tracks View

Another powerful feature is ACID's ability to show the Bus Tracks view. In this window, which appears beneath the main track view, you are allowed to automate parameters relating to a bus, including volume, panning, and any automated FX routed to a bus. By routing a group of tracks to a single bus, you are allowed to control that group of tracks' volume all at once using the Bus Tracks view.

By default, this view is off. You can enable or disable the view by pressing B on your keyboard.

You don't want to go overboard. Reverse only small portions of an event, like the second or fourth beat.

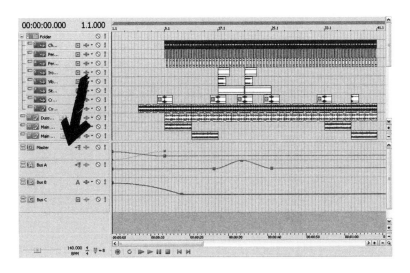

Create a Natural Chorus Effect

While it's true that you can use the Chorus plug-in to create a chorus effect, you can save some processing power by creating your own natural-sounding chorus effect. This technique comes in handy for tracks that contain similar material.

To create a natural-sounding chorus effect:

1. Click to place the cursor on the Timeline where you'd like to create the chorus effect between two (or more) tracks.

2. Zoom in on the Timeline all the way. A quick way of doing this is to hold Ctrl while pressing the Up Arrow key. You may have to readjust the track view vertically to get the track you need.

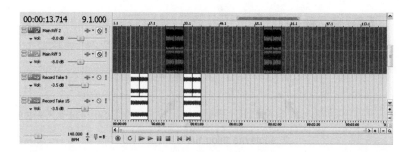

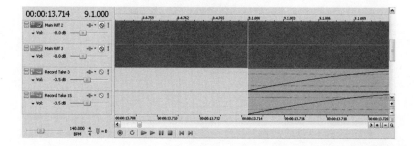

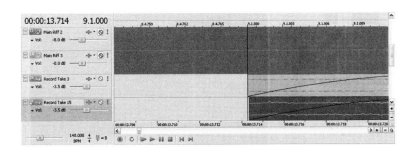

3. Click a track's event and then press 4 or 6 on your keyboard's numeric keypad to nudge the track's event pixel by pixel. About three times should do it.

Pan one track hard left and the other hard right for a more pronounced effect.

The "Wall of Sound" Effect

By layering multiple tracks of different (or similar) instruments or sounds all at once, a dense, rich sonic project can emerge, creating the famous Phil Spector "Wall of Sound™" effect first made famous back in the 60's.

You can do the same by recording the same part over a few times and then layering them together for a great, thick sound. Creating a project with multiple tracks that weave in and out of each other can also produce the same effect.

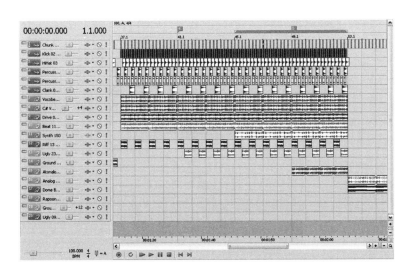

Pitch-Shifting Tracks

In addition to layering tracks together, you can change the pitch of the events or tracks so that they harmonize with other events and tracks, creating interest in the listener.

See chapter 17, "Useful Formulas and Aids for ACID," for tips on harmonizing your pitch-shifted tracks.

To pitch-shift an event:

1. Click the event on the Timeline.

2. Press the + or – keys on your keyboard's numeric keypad to pitch-shift the event in semitones.

To pitch-shift an entire track:

1. Click the track in the track list.

2. Press the + or – keys on your keyboard's numeric keypad to pitch-shift the event in semitones.

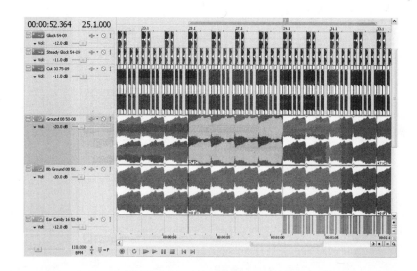

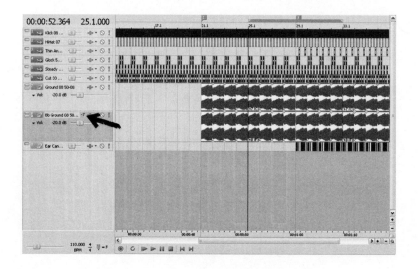

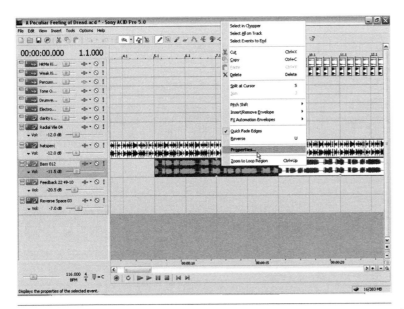

Detuning Tracks

Detuning involves taking a copied track and slightly placing the copied track out of tune, giving the effect that the copied track itself is different from the original.

To detune an event:

1. Right-click an event on the Timeline and choose Properties.

2. In the Event Properties window, enter a value in cents rather than semitones under "Pitch shift (semitones)."

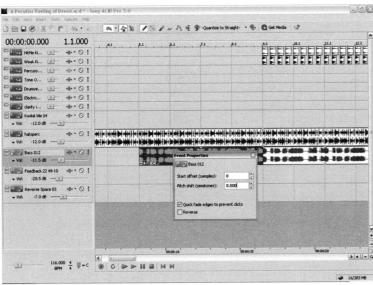

To detune an entire track:

1. Double-click a track's icon in the track list.

2. In the General tab in the Track Properties window, enter a value in cents rather than semitones under "Pitch shift (semitones)."

Employing Other Creative Tricks

You can also use ACID to achieve other studio techniques, like panning a "dry" track (a track with no effects) hard left and panning the same track with effects (also called a "wet" track) hard right.

You can create a spooky, ghostly reverse reverb effect with ACID by using its reverse event function:

1. Click a track's event on the Timeline.

2. Solo the track (X on your keyboard).

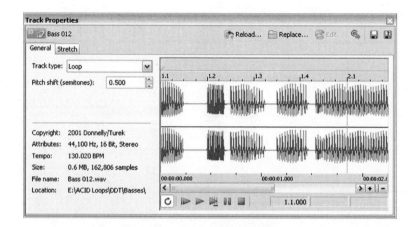

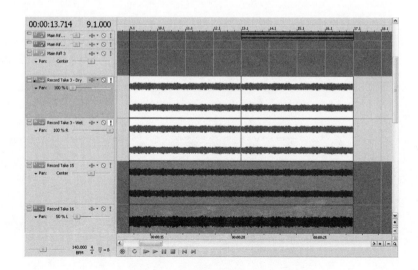

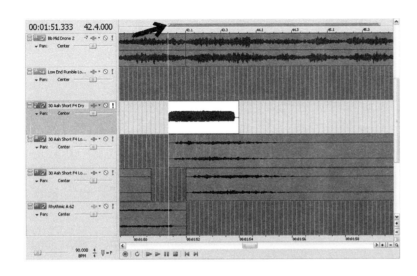

3. Place the Loop Region over the beginning of the event and two or three measures after the event.

4. Click the Track FX button in the corresponding track in the track list.

5. Click the Edit Chain button.

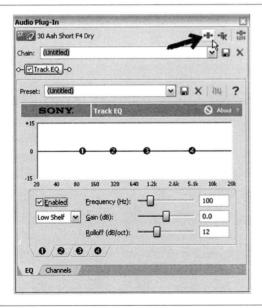

6. In the Plug-In Chooser window, select the Sony folder and then double-click the Reverb plug-in.

7. Click OK.

8. Select a Reverb preset like "Cathedral" or create your own. Give the setting plenty of reverb and decay.

9. Close the window.

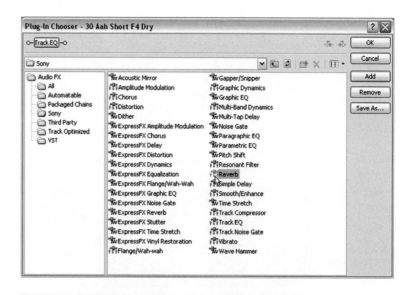

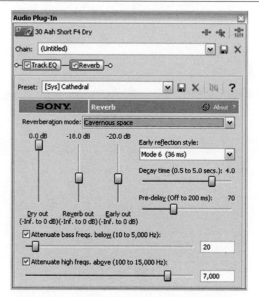

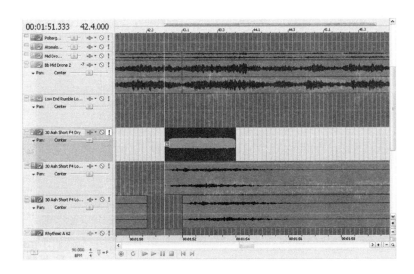

10. Click the event and press U on your keyboard to reverse the event.

11. Render the event to a new track by pressing Ctrl+M and check the option "Render loop region only."

12. Click the Save button.

Be sure to set the soloed tracks to unity (0.0 dBFS) before rendering to a new track.

13. Once the track renders, mute the original track and then paint the new track's event in its entirety using the Paint Tool while holding down Ctrl and clicking on the new track's Timeline. Line the event's end up with the event's end of the original track.

14. Press U to reverse the event.

15. Play back the new track.

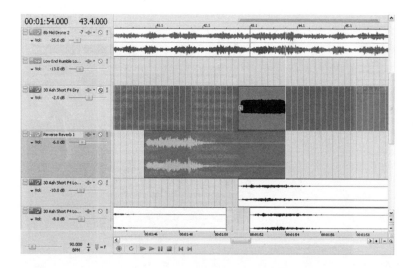

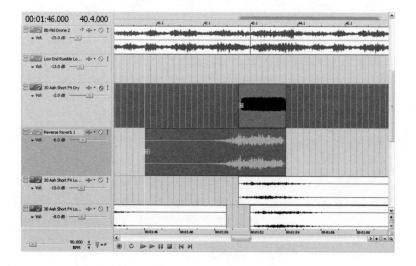

Chapter 5

Beatmapping Existing Songs

Beatmapping is the process of mapping the beat of a song to ACID tempo information. It is accomplished with the ACID Beatmapper. The Beatmapper adds information to the project or the song that identifies the first downbeat and the duration of a measure. From these two pieces of information, ACID calculates the beats per minute (bpm) and maps the song's tempo. Once a song is beatmapped, it will follow the tempo of the project, and any loop that you bring into ACID will map to the beat of the song as well. This is the heart of remixing songs to create things like a "mash-up"—a track that uses vocals from one song superimposed over the backing tracks of another.

Sometimes beatmapping is used to create an entirely new song that feels like another song. This allows you to use a song as a "template" so that you can mimic its feel while adding loops of your own. In the end, you remove the original song and are left with something similar but new. Finally, you might have purchased some royalty-free music that you have used on several projects and now you want to give it a new sound by adding some loops or rearranging the parts so that it fits better within your particular project.

Know Your Copyrights

A proper review of copyright law is well beyond the scope of this book, but it is important to understand when you may be violating someone else's copyrights. If you bring a song into ACID for which you are not the copyright owner and you change it by rearranging the parts, or adding additional content, you have created a derivative work. If you plan to play back this work in public or use it on a project that is not for your own personal use, or it doesn't fall under fair use, you may be violating someone's copyright.

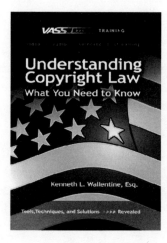

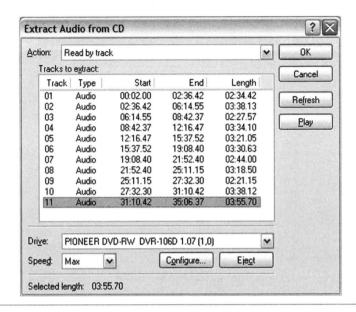

Extracting Audio from CDs

The first step in beatmapping is to acquire the song. ACID has the tools to extract songs from CDs and place them onto your hard drive for you.

To extract a song from a CD:

1. Place the CD you want to extract audio from in your CD or DVD drive.

2. Select File>Extract Audio from CD.

3. Make sure "Read by track" is selected.

4. In the Extract Audio from CD dialog box, select the track or tracks that you want to extract.

5. Optionally, click the Play button to audition the songs before making your final selection.

6. Click OK when you have found the track you want to extract.

7. In the Save As dialog, make sure choose a directory you want the track to be saved to and give the file a name you can remember.

8. Click OK.

While the default setting in this dialog is to "Read by track," you can also select "Read entire disk" to read all the tracks and "Read by range" to select a subset of the disc by time interval.

Matching Tempo

Once the track has been extracted, the Beatmapper dialog will automatically appear if you have "Automatically start the Beatmapper Wizard for long files" selected in your preferences (this is the default). The dialog gives you the option of saying Yes or No to start beatmapping. Leave Yes selected and click Next.

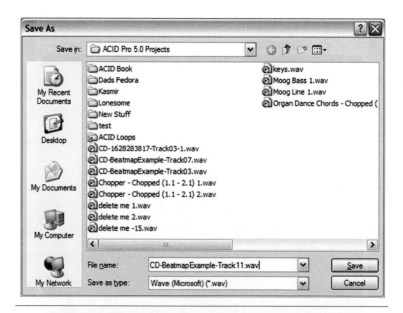

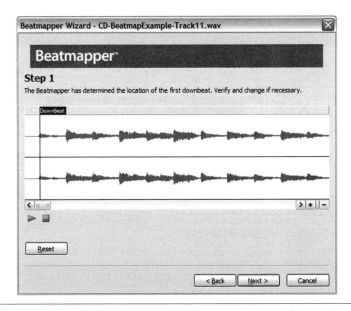

You should now see the Beatmapper Step 1 dialog box. This dialog box allows you to set the initial downbeat. ACID will try to guess where the first downbeat is, but this may need changing depending on how the song begins and whether or not the beginning follows the beat of the song. While it is critical to find the correct downbeat, it is not necessary for you to get it right in this step. The next step will still allow you to fine tune the initial downbeat, so just try to get it as close as you can at this stage to make the next stage easier. Click Next when you are done.

Use the zoom in and out buttons or your mouse wheel to zoom into the waveform. This will help you determine where to place the downbeat and end measure.

In Step 2 of the Beatmapper you must specifying the duration of one measure which will define the beats per minute of the song. The best way to do this is to click Play and adjust the end point of the measure until the clicks of the metronome and the accompanying vertical beat lines line up with the beats of the measure. Use the waveform as your guide. Downbeats are usually accompanied by percussion that creates spikes in the waveform. These spikes can often be used to align to the beat. **Note:** You can beatmap songs only in 4/4 time.

In Step 3 of the Beatmapper you can check how closely your tempo maps to the rest of the song. Use the arrow keys that are next to the Measure slider to advance your beatmap to the next and previous measure. Does it still sound like it's on tempo? If yes, check the next measure, if not go back to Step 2 and adjust the measure again. You cannot adjust the length of the measure in Step 3. You must go back to Step 2 for that. Step 3 will only slip edit the measure start, keeping the duration constant. You will know that you have the beatmapping correct when you can move the measure selector out to the fifth or sixth measure in Step 3 and the beat is still on tempo. If you can't get the song to beatmap properly, it may be because the song is not at a constant tempo. See the Fixing Tempo Drift Using ACID section of this chapter for ways to fix this. Click Next to continue.

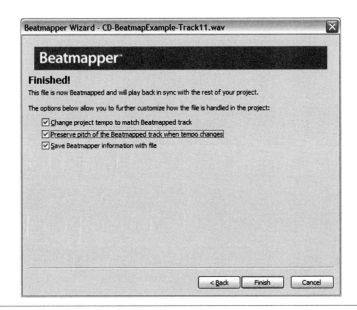

In the Finished step, the hard work is complete. You have three options to select from:

1. **Change project tempo to match Beatmapped track.** This is probably a good idea if you want the song you are beatmapping to be played at its original tempo. If, however, you want the beatmapped track to match the current project tempo, uncheck this option, and the track will play at the project tempo instead.

2. **Preserve pitch of the beatmapped track when tempo changes.** I like to check this one because it allows the beatmapped track to play at the same pitch even when the tempo changes, as if the musicians were speeding up and slowing down, which is what would naturally happen. If you want the beatmapped track to change pitch when it speeds up (like spinning a record faster), then leave this unchecked.

3. **Save beatmapper information with the file.** This is a personal preference, and I like to keep it checked. It adds metadata to the file so that the beatmap can be used in other projects. If you uncheck this box, the beatmap information will be stored with the current project only.

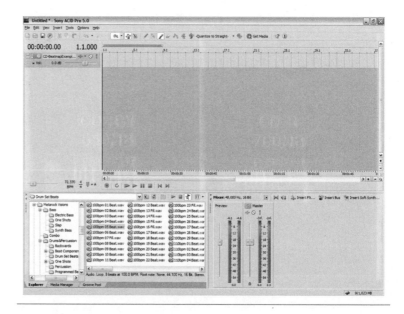

These three options can be changed later in the Track Properties dialog, so don't worry too much about getting them right the first time. Over time, you will get a better feel for how to set them for the particular project you are working on. Click the Finish button to complete the Beatmapper.

Congratulations, you have beatmapped your first track. But where's the music? Remember, ACID does not play any sounds just because a track is inserted into the project. You have to paint events on the track where you want music to play.

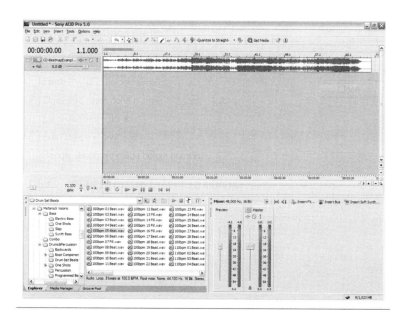

You can now use the Draw Tool (Ctrl+D) to draw the song on the track. If you want the whole beatmapped song to play, take the Paint Tool and hold the Ctrl key while you click at the beginning of the track (or wherever you want the beatmapped song to start playing), and the entire song will be inserted into the track without having to paint all the measures. If you just want to add sections of the song you can use the S key to split the song into sections and then move those sections around or delete the selections you don't want.

Use the Ctrl key with the Paint Tool to instantly paint a loop, one-shot, or beatmapper track for its entire duration.

Knowing When to Start

Finding the downbeat can be difficult at times, but if you can tap in time to the music, you can find the downbeat using the following method. An interesting feature of the Beatmapper is that it will stop playing the song and place the downbeat marker when the Enter key is pressed. If the song has an introduction that is not in tempo, you should listen to it a few times in the Beatmapper Step 1 dialog to get a feel for when the first measure after the introduction starts. Tap along with the beat on your knee or desk first. Remember, the downbeat is the first beat of the measure. If the song is in 4/4 time, the downbeat is on the 1 of each 1-2-3-4 beat count. Listen to the song and try to anticipate when the first beat will be. At that point, press the Enter key to stop the music on the downbeat. Then zoom in on the wave display and fine-tune the downbeat marker to start at the beginning of the first beat.

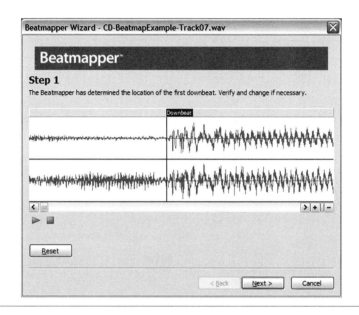

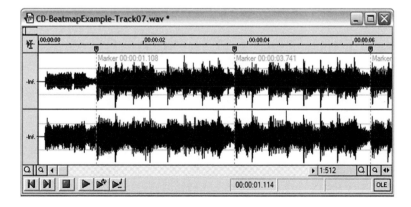

Sometimes you can see the downbeat in the wave file shape because it causes a spike. Don't be fooled by songs that start with a pick-up note (also called an upbeat). A pick-up note is when a song starts on the third or fourth beat of the previous measure. You may hear a live band count: 1-2-3 and start playing on the 4.

When all else fails, you may have to use a tool like Sound Forge to tap markers on the beats as the song plays. If you miss the initial beat, use the distance between the other markers as a guide. Then calculate backwards to the missing markers at the beginning of the song to find where the downbeat of the first measure should be.

You can beatmap the file right in Sound Forge using the ACID Properties. Select ACID 3.0 Beatmapped as the ACID type before you save the file in Sound Forge.

Fixing Tempo Drift Using ACID

Tempo drift happens when a song is not recorded at a steady tempo. Some musicians record to a "click track" in the studio, but many do not, especially if they are trying to get a "live" feel. Although most good drummers can keep a steady beat, they will eventually drift against the steady clock of your computer, and the song slowly drifts out of tempo. There is no automatic way to fix this. It is a time-consuming manual process.

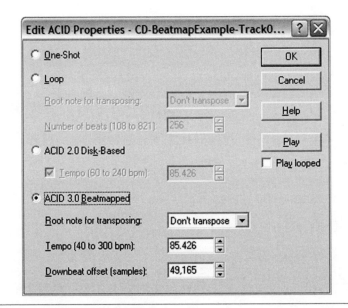

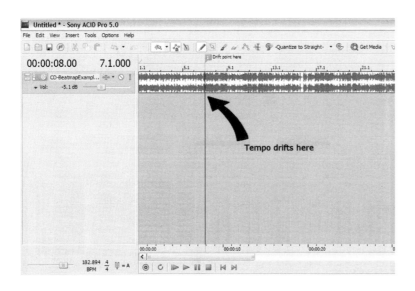

To fix tempo drift in ACID, you should Beatmap the file as described in the Matching Tempos section of this book, but follow these two rules when you get to the Beatmapper's Finish dialog box:

- Check "Preserve pitch of the Beatmapped track when tempo changes" because you don't want the pitch of the song to change as you change the beatmap.

- Uncheck "Save Beatmapper information with the file" because you will be beatmapping the same file several times and if saved in the file, this information will overwrite the previous information which is needed for the other copies on other tracks.

After you beatmap the song the first time, play the song on the Timeline using the metronome until you hear it drift off beat. Split the track at this point using the S key, and delete the remainder of the song on the track. Drop the original file onto a lower track and start the Beatmapper process again but, this time place the down-beat at the place the song drifted off tempo.

Keep repeating this procedure until the end of the song and save the beatmap information with the ACID project only (not in the file). It will take time and patience, but it can be done. When finished, render all those tracks to a new track and delete the old tracks from the project. What you have left should be a consistently beatmapped song.

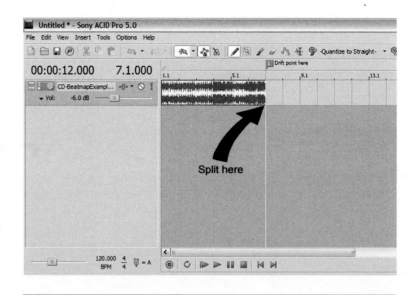

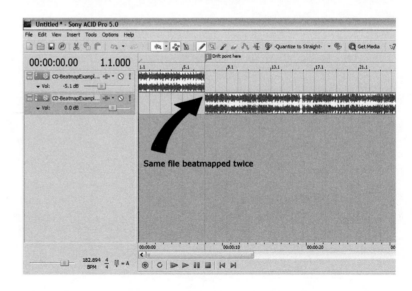

Chapter 6

Advanced Looping

There's more to ACID than just "pick, paint and play." This chapter outlines several techniques that will help you get more out of ACID's vast power for manipulating loops.

Manipulating Loops

To change the tempo of a loop track:

1. Access the track's properties by double-clicking the track's icon in the track list.

2. Under the Stretch tab, double the value under "Number of beats" to halve the tempo; halve the value to double the tempo.

Keep halving or doubling the number of beats if the tempo of the track still doesn't give you the results that you need.

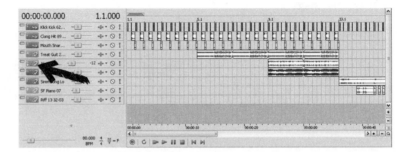

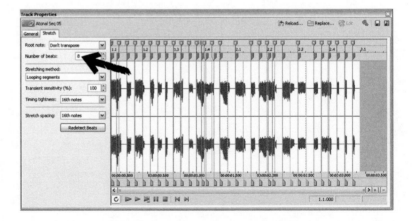

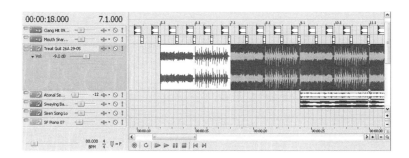

To split an event:

1. Click a track's event on the Timeline and to place the cursor where you want the split to occur. (You may toggle snapping by pressing F8 on your keyboard.)

2. Press S on your keyboard. The event now splits into two events.

To join events:

1. Click the events on the track that you want to join together.

2. Press J on your keyboard. The events join together.

The first event in the Timeline will be the basis for joining the events together. You can also use the Paint Tool to join events. Whatever event the Paint Tool touches first will become the basis for joining events.

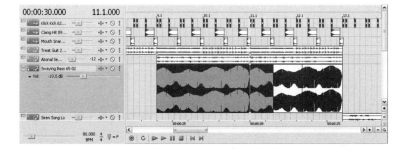

To insert quick fades on overlapping events between two tracks:

1. Select the events that are overlapping between tracks on the Timeline.

   Right-click the quick fade edges and choose Fade Type to choose different quick-fade edges.

2. Press F on your keyboard. Quick fade edges appear on the events.

Reversing Events

To reverse an event:

1. Click the event on the Timeline.

2. Press U on your keyboard to reverse the event. An icon appears to let you know the event was reversed.

You may also select multiple events and reverse them all at once.

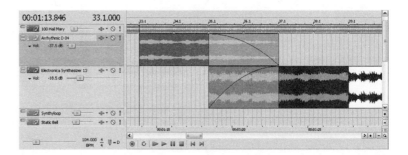

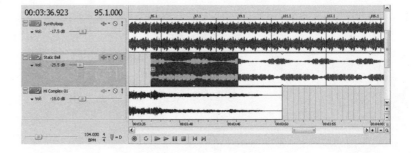

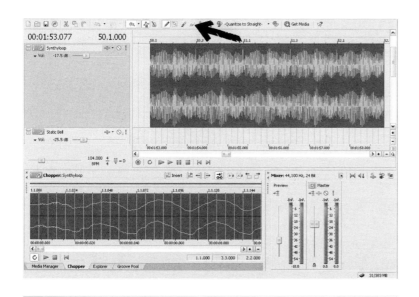

Pseudo-Granular Synthesis/ Stutter Effect

To produce a stutter effect very much like granular synthesis:

1. Zoom in on an event. Select a grid resolution double that of the stutter duration you intend to create. (For example, select 16th note resolution to create 8th note stuttering.)

2. Click the Erase Tool button on ACID's toolbar.

3. Click every other space on the grid to erase the event's contents.

Ensure snapping is on by pressing F8 on your keyboard.

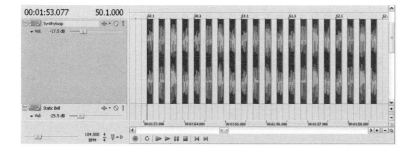

The Paint Tool and One-Shots

You can use the Paint Tool coupled with one-shots to "program" a sequence of events. This is a great way to create percussion tracks of your own rhythmic design.

To paint a track using one-shots:

1. Click the drop-down arrow next to the Enable Snapping button on ACID's toolbar. Set the grid resolution to a desired note value.

2. Click the Paint Tool button and, while holding down Ctrl on your keyboard, click and drag across a one-shot track's Timeline.

3. Change the grid resolution as necessary to change to other note values as you paint.

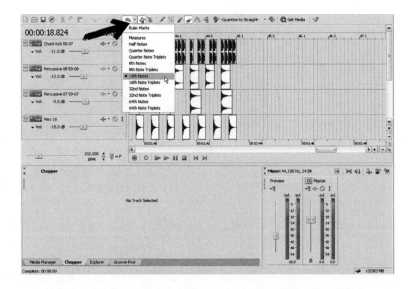

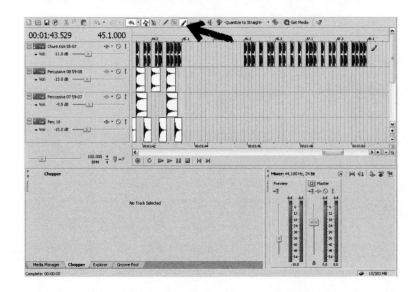

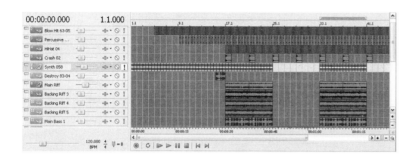

Rendering FX with a Track

Rendering FX with a track will save you some processing power your system could use for other tasks in ACID, rather than ACID having to employ FX in real time. Some applications call this process "freezing the track."

You can either render the entire track or only a portion of the track.

To render the FX with an entire track:

1. Solo the track with FX by clicking the track's icon in the track list and pressing X on your keyboard.

2. Render to a new track using Ctrl+M on your keyboard. Name your new track and press Save.

Paint the newly rendered track's contents in by using the Paint Tool and holding down Ctrl on your keyboard while painting.

Remember that the length of the rendered audio will determine what kind of ACIDized track type it will become. See chapter 9, ACIDized Track Types, and, ACIDization of Rendered Loops, for more info.

To render the FX with a portion of a track:

1. Solo the track with FX by clicking the track and pressing X on your keyboard

2. Set the Loop Region over just the area you'd like to keep by clicking and dragging across the Marker Bar

3. Render to a new track using CTRL+M on your keyboard. Check the Render loop region only option. Name your new track and press Save.

Be sure to get the soloed track's volume as close to unity (0.0 dBFS) as possible before rendering, then mix the newly rendered track with the rest of your project afterwards.

Remember that the length of the rendered audio will determine what kind of ACIDized track type it will become. See chapter 9, "ACIDized Track Types," and, "ACIDization of Rendered Loops," for more info.

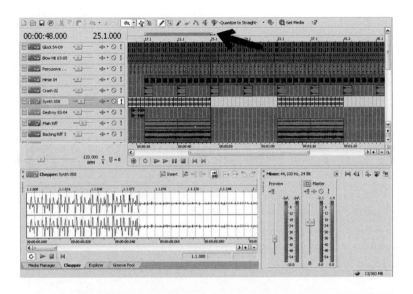

Chapter 7

Grooving to the Beat!

Sometimes you feel as if your projects are a little too cold or mechanical, or something sounds "off." Groove quantization can massage your projects by giving them a human feel or helping an off-kilter recording sound a little more in time rhythmically. This is an exciting new feature of ACID 5 worthy of special mention.

Applying Grooves

To apply a groove to a track:

1. Click the drop-down arrow next to the Groove Tool button on the toolbar and choose a groove from the list.

2. Click and drag over an event on the Timeline. The event will shrink a bit vertically to accommodate the groove. You can see the groove being painted at the bottom of the event.

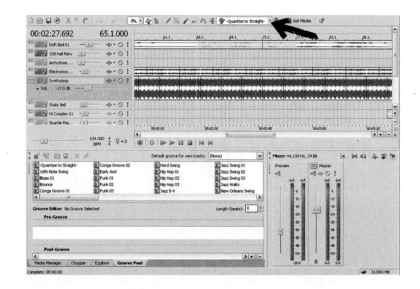

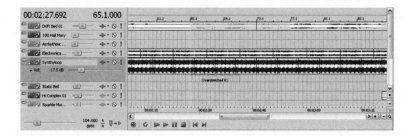

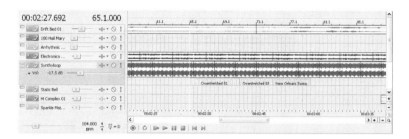

3. Repeat if desired to apply different grooves to multiple events on the same track.

You can also drag a groove from the Groove Pool to the space between two groove events to achieve the same technique.

To erase a groove from a track:

With the Groove Tool active, right-click on a groove event to erase the contents underneath the tool.

Erasing, like painting, "snaps" to the nearest grid resolution. Toggle snapping by pressing F8 on your keyboard or temporarily disable snapping by pressing and holding down Shift while erasing or painting.

Hold down Ctrl while clicking between two groove events to fill the empty space between the events with another groove.

Apply a groove to the entire track by holding down Ctrl while painting across the track. Erase an entire groove by holding down Ctrl while right-clicking.

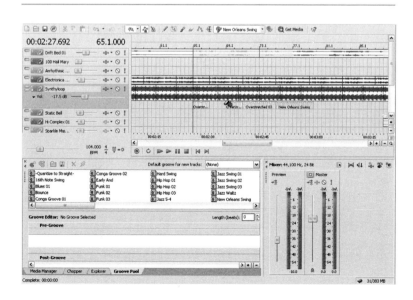

The Groove Pool

The Groove Pool is where you can create, duplicate, import, export, and remove grooves, as well as tweak new and existing grooves using the Groove Editor.

To create a new groove:

1. Open the Groove Pool using Ctrl+Alt+7 on your keyboard.

2. Click the New Groove button.

3. Rename the groove by right-clicking the groove and choosing Rename. (By default, the new groove is called "New Groove.")

Duplicating grooves allows you to tweak existing grooves while leaving the original alone.

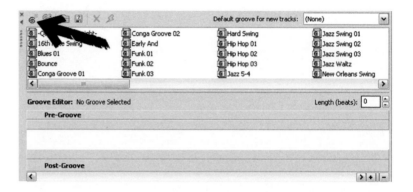

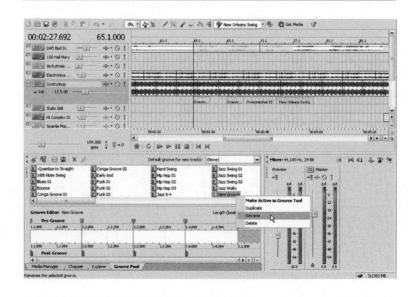

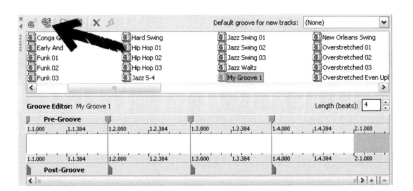

To duplicate a groove:

1. Click a groove in the Groove Pool.

2. Click the Duplicate Selected Grooves button.

3. Rename a duplicated groove by right-clicking it and selecting Rename. Duplicated grooves are named "Copy of ...".

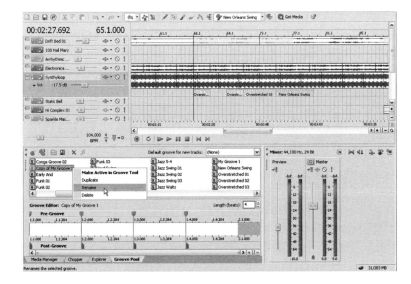

To import a groove:

1. Click the Import Groove button in the Groove Pool.

When importing media files instead of groove files, ACID takes the autodetected beat info and uses that for the groove.

2. Browse to a groove or a media file.

3. Click Open.

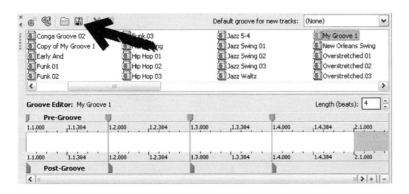

You can export grooves, especially custom grooves, for the purposes of sharing and archiving.

To export a groove:

1. Click a groove in the Groove Pool. Click the Export Groove button.

2. Give your groove a name or keep the existing name.

3. Click Save.

You can also export custom grooves for use in other projects, as custom grooves won't appear in other projects unless you save the custom groove as a .groove file.

The default folder for groove files is C:\Program Files\Sony\ACID Pro 5.0\Grooves\. This can be changed by going to the Folders tab under Options> Preferences.

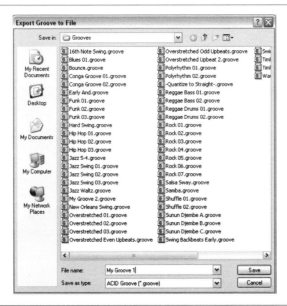

The Groove Editor

The Groove Editor is where you'll do all the tweaking for your groove. You can add, modify, or delete beat anchors and groove markers here, as well as change the length in number of beats the groove will be.

Beat anchors represent the actual beats you want to adjust, while the groove markers represent where you want them to play. A beat anchor has a corresponding groove marker, and a line is drawn between them to indicate this relationship.

To add a beat anchor and its corresponding groove marker:

1. Click where you want the beat anchor and groove marker to appear in the Groove Editor.

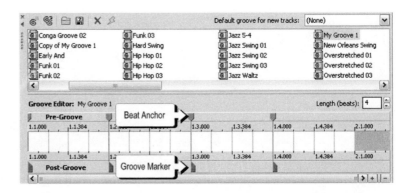

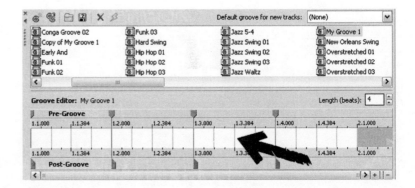

2. Press M on your keyboard.

To adjust a beat anchor or groove marker, click and drag the appropriate anchor or marker. You cannot drag beat anchors or stretch markers past each other.

It may help to toggle snapping by pressing F8 on your keyboard to precisely place an anchor and marker.

Since beat anchors themselves snap to the nearest grid resolution, you can either press F8 to disable snapping or hold down Shift while dragging to temporarily disable snapping.

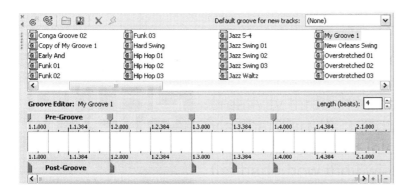

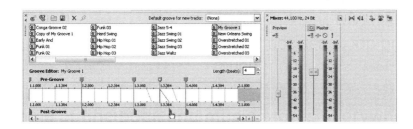

To adjust the length of a groove, change the value in the Length (beats) field in the Groove Editor.

The Groove Editor and the Properties of a Loop Track

If you've gone into a loop track's properties, you may have noticed that under the Stretch tab there's a similar interface to that of the Groove Editor when working with grooves. The groove you create and edit in the track properties will be the groove used when using the "Quantize to Straight" groove in the Groove Pool. Using other grooves will override the groove created in the track properties.

The blue beat anchors always represent the quantized version of the loop. The markers (green or red) are what do the opposite. In the Groove Editor, you have blue mapping to red. If you apply that groove to a quantized file, it will slide those previously quantized notes around to create the groove sound.

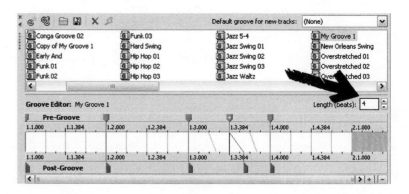

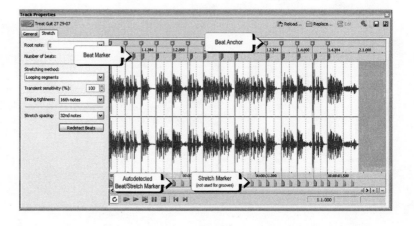

In the track properties, the green and orange markers are marking your transient attacks, which also translates into where the attacks are as grooved. The beat anchors above them show where you would want the transients to be if you removed your groove and quantized the file.

When you clone your groove to the groove pool, it takes those quantized beat anchors and makes them the "pre-groove" quantized markers. All of your transient attacks which were marked as green are noted at the same positions in red—now signifying where the quantized notes should move to.

Groove Cloning

You can export the existing groove of a loop track to the Groove Pool for further refining and adding to other tracks.

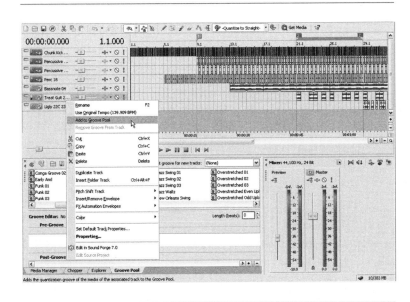

To add a groove to the Groove Pool:

1. Right-click a Loop track and choose Add to Groove Pool.

You can also use the Add to Groove Pool button in the track properties.

2. The quantized groove is added to the Groove Pool, ready for you to edit.

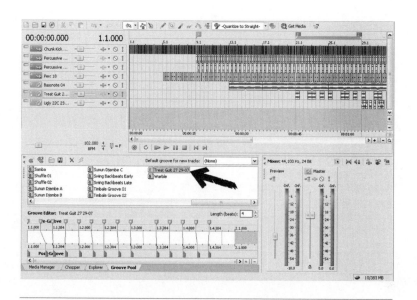

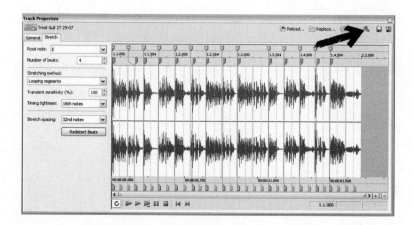

Chapter 8

Organization Techniques

It goes without saying that organization is key to getting your projects done with minimal effort. This chapter outlines some techniques and features you can use in ACID to help you organize your projects more efficiently.

Using Track Colors to Organize

Using track colors will help you easily identify and group parts of a project for easier organization.

To change the color of a track:

1. Right-click the track's icon in the track list.

2. Select Color from the context menu.

3. Choose a color from the pop-up menu.

You may also select multiple tracks using the standard Windows method for selecting files, then changing all their colors at once to one specific color using the method above.

You may also customize the colors of tracks, up to eight different colors:

1. Select Options>Preferences on ACID's menu bar.

2. Click the Display tab.

3. Choose a track color letter and then click the color swatch to adjust the color.

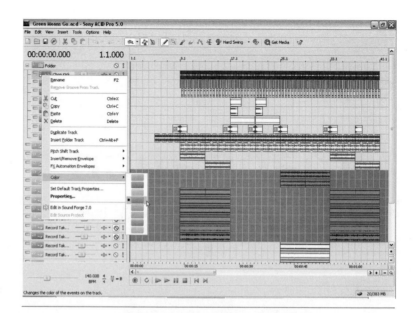

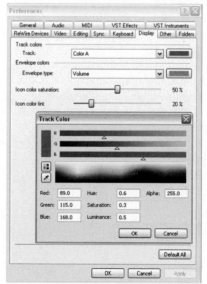

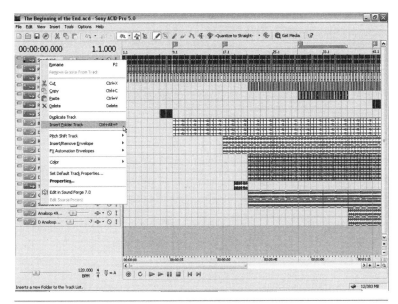

Using Folders Tracks to Organize and Edit

You can create folder tracks for your project to help you more easily categorize tracks. This is especially handy for projects with many tracks. You could create a folder track just for percussion and another for guitar, or create a folder track for a song's verse while another contains a chorus.

To create a folder track:

1. Right-click the track in the track list where you want the folder track to appear. The folder track will be inserted underneath the active, selected track.

2. Select Insert Folder Track from the Context menu. You can also highlight the track and use Ctrl+Alt+F on your keyboard or select Insert> Folder Track from the main menu.

3. Give the folder track a new name by double-clicking the scribble sheet and typing a name. Press Enter when done.

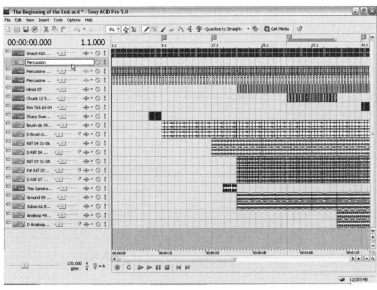

You can then begin to drag tracks into this new folder track. To drag a track into a folder track:

1. Click and drag a track into the track folder.

If you have a group of tracks already in a folder track and you drag another track into the folder, you can specify where you want to place the track in the group:

1. Click and drag a track into the group of tracks in the folder, but don't release the mouse button. The folder track will highlight to let you know the track will be placed in the folder, and a highlight will appear to let you know where the track will be placed in the group.

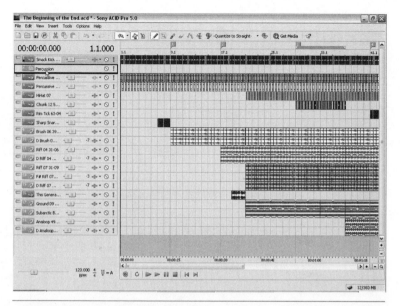

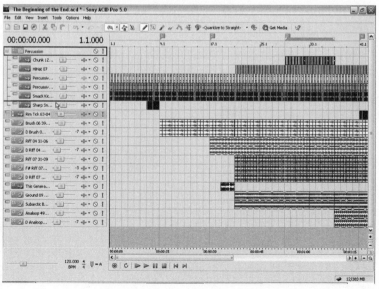

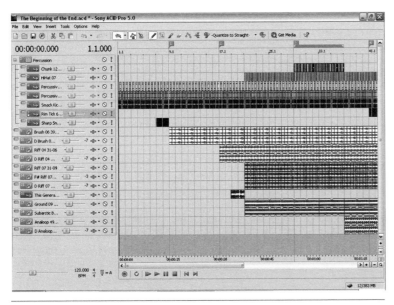

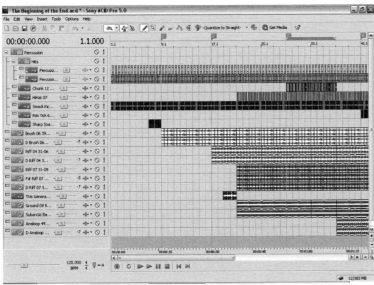

2. Release the mouse button. The track is then inserted within the group.

To move multiple tracks, hold down Shift while clicking to select a sequential number of tracks. Hold down Ctrl while clicking to select nonsequential tracks. Drag the tracks into the folder track when done.

You may even nest a folder track within another folder track using the same methods you would for other tracks.

Folder tracks may be muted and soloed just like any other track. The added bonus is that you only need to mute or solo the one folder track, rather than having to select an entire group of tracks one by one.

You may also use the conventional Windows methods for selecting and moving groups of sequentially and nonsequentially selected tracks into a folder track.

Customize Media Folders

You can specify a single folder for multiple projects or multiple folders for multiple projects, as well as specify folders for your groove files made with the Groove Pool. You can also specify different folders for different types of media saves. For example, you can specify a folder for project renders and a separate folder for recordings.

When you specify a single folder, all of your projects, as well as any related media, will default to the single folder. Everything, including ACD and ACD-ZIP project files, MIDI files, renders, and newly rendered and chopped tracks will go into this folder.

To specify a single folder for all your projects and related media:

1. Select Options>Preferences from the menu bar.

2. Click the Folders tab.

3. Select the option "Use a single default folder for project media saves."

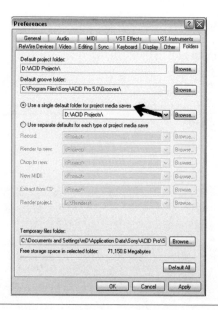

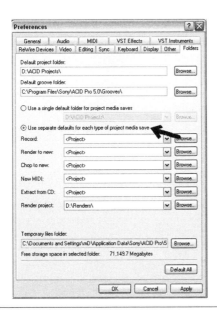

4. Click the Browse button to browse to a preferred folder.

5. Click OK.

When you specify multiple folders, your projects and any related media saves may be placed in separate folders for easier organization. This is probably a better option for those who like to micromanage their projects. You won't have to go fishing through an entire folder to find the related media to the project.

To specify different folders for your projects and related media:

1. Select Options>Preferences on the menu bar.

2. Click the Folders tab.

3. Select the option "Use separate defaults for each type of media save."

4. Click the Browse button next to each respective type of media save, and browse to a specific folder for that media save.

5. Click OK.

When you first save your project in a preferred location, you can tell ACID to also save any related media such as recordings to the same location as the project file. To do that, you would select <Project> in the menu drop-down box instead of browsing to a specific folder for each type of media save.

Save the ACID project file in a specific folder before doing any media saving tasks. This will ensure that any related media will stay with the project.

Media Manager

Since using very large media libraries can introduce a performance hit on your system, you're better off creating smaller libraries instead of one huge library.

The Media Manager is a new feature in ACID Pro that lets you organize and search your collection of loops and samples to find the right media for your ACID project. You can also preview and add files to your ACID project in the same manner that you use the Explorer.

The Media Manager uses media libraries to organize your media. You can create as many libraries as you'd like.

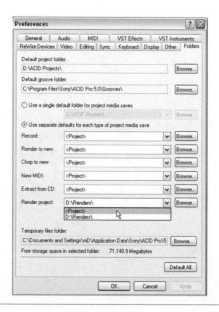

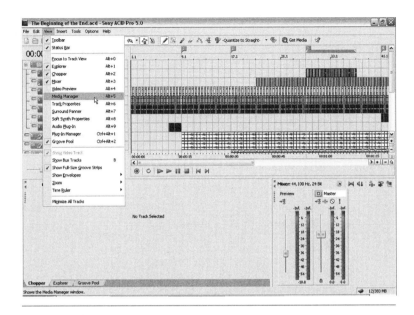

By default, media relating to a project is automatically added to your media library every time you open a project. This is so ACID creates relationships between media based on such criteria as which media was used at the same time in a project. If you don't care to use this feature, you can turn it off by going to Options>Preferences and then under the General tab and uncheck the option "Save media-usage relationships in active media library." Alternately, you could create a library expressly for the purpose of media usage relation-ships.

To create a media library:

1. Select the menu item View>Media Manager or press Alt+5 on your keyboard.

2. Click the Media Library Actions button and choose New Media Library.

3. Give your library a name and click Create.

The new library is then created and opened in the Media Manager, ready for you to add media files to your library and tag and classify your media files.

You'll next want to add media files to your library so that you may work with them in the Media Manager. To add files to your library:

1. Click the Add Files to Media Library button.

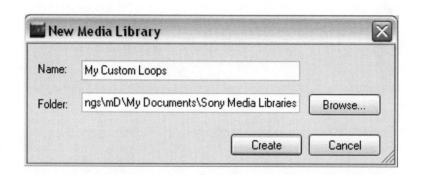

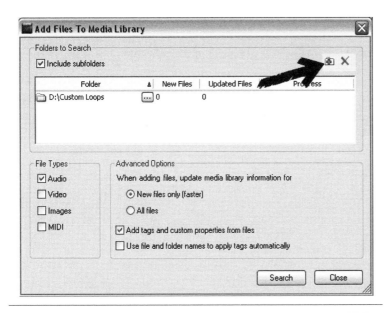

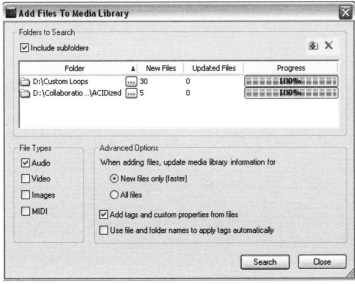

2. In the Add Files to Media Library window, click the Add Folder button in the upper right to browse for a folder to search for media.

3. Click OK. Repeat for any folders you want to add to the search.

4. When ready, click the Search button.

5. Once the search completes, click the Close button to add the media to the library.

The best way to organize media using the Media Manager is to use tags. Tags will also help find your desired media faster than using the conventional search method.

If you ever update info for particular media (like changing ACIDized properties for media), be sure to use the "When adding files, update media library information for: All files" option under Advanced Options.

To assign a tag to media:

1. Select media in the library. You may use the conventional Windows methods for selecting files.

2. Select a tag in the tag tree, then drag the tag over to the media. You will see the media highlight as well as the cursor to change to reflect that the tag will be applied to the media.

3. Release the mouse button. A tag is now applied to the media. Now that the tag is assigned to the media, checking the checkbox next to the assigned tag in the tag tree will bring up that media only.

You can tag your media with multiple tags.

You may also tag your media using multiple tags. Use the conventional Windows methods for selecting files to select multiple tags, and then drag the tags over to the selected media.

If you have decided that you don't want a certain tag applied to media, you may also easily remove a tag from the media.

To remove a tag:

In the tag tree window, click the Remove Tag Mode button.

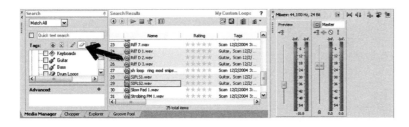

1. With the media selected in the Search Results window, click the tag you'd like to remove from the media in the tag tree.

2. Drag the tag over to the media and release the mouse button. The tag should then be removed.

You can also add your own tags to the tag tree. To add a tag to the tag tree:

1. In the tag tree window, select where you want the tag to appear in the tree.

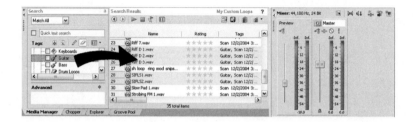

2. Click the Add Tag button and the tag will appear in the tag tree.

3. Give your tag a name and press Enter on your keyboard.

You can then proceed to tag your media with this new tag or create tags within this tag.

You can use the Media Manager all by itself to organize your collection, but if you already have a bevy of Sony loop collections, the Sony Sound Series Loops and Samples Reference Library will definitely help. The Sony Loops and Samples Reference Library will automatically tag any Sony collections you may have so you won't have to, saving you a lot of time in organizing your Sony loop collections.

You must download and install the Sony Loops and Samples Reference Library if you want to automatically tag your Sony media. You can pick up the Sony Sound Series Loops and Samples Reference Library at: http://mediasoftware.sonypictures.com/reference.

To use the Sony Sound Series Loops
and Samples Reference Library:

1. Press the Media Library Actions but-
    ton in the Media Manager and select
    Options.

2. Under Reference Library, click the
    drop-down menu and select Sony
    Sound Series Loops and Samples.

3. Click OK.

Now when any Sony media is added to
your library, it will be automatically
tagged.

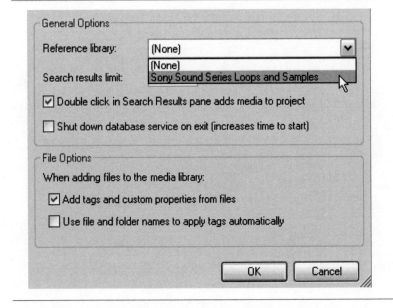

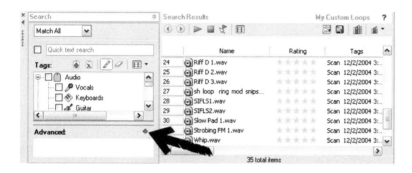

If there's a very specific type of media that you want to find or use, you can use the Media Manager's advanced search feature to find the media you need:

1. In the Media Manager window, click the Add New Search Criteria button.

2. Drag the criteria you wish to filter to the Advanced section and release.

3. Specify parameters for your criteria by clicking the default parameter and choosing parameters from a list or entering a numerical value depending on the parameter.

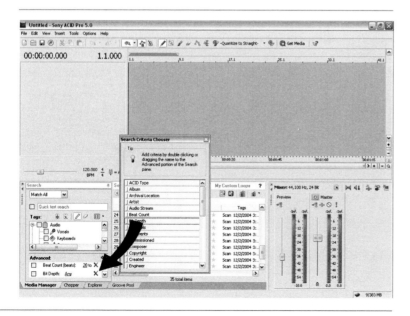

4. When done setting parameters, check the box next to the criteria in the list to search for that media. Uncheck to exclude. The specified media appears in the search results window

You can also click the Find Related Media button in the search results window to quickly find related media and add it to the advanced section. For example, clicking the button for a beat count of 8 will find all related media in that library.

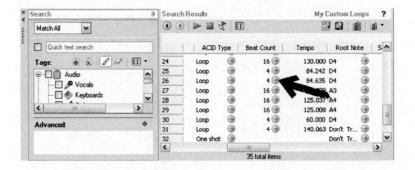

Chapter 9

Creating Your Own Loops

Part of ACID's power is the ability to create your own loops, whether they be from existing content or your own content. This chapter will outline several different techniques that will not only let you create your own loops but also ACIDize them, a process that will add a chunk of data to your samples so that they will time-stretch to any tempo and key-stretch to any key properly.

Choping to a New Track Using the Chopper

To chop to a new track using the Chopper:

1. Bring up the Chopper window by pressing Alt+2 on your keyboard.

2. Click and drag on the waveform to make a selection.

3. Right-click the selection and select Chop to New Track.

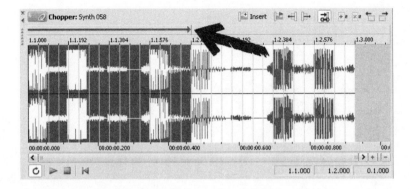

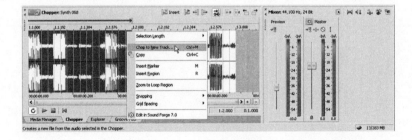

4. Give the new track a name (or accept the default)

5. Click Save.

The newly chopped track will then be added to your project.

You may also make a selection in the Chopper by doing any of the following:

- Right-click the waveform and select Selection Length, and then choose a selection length.

- Hold down Shift while clicking and dragging, which turns snapping off. This is a good technique to use if you need a more precise selection.

Recorded takes have regions automatically applied to them for each measure. These regions show up in both the track's properties and in the Chopper. The regions also show up in an external audio editor such as Sound Forge. This makes it very easy to distinguish what you want from the take, construct a new arrangement, and discard the rest.

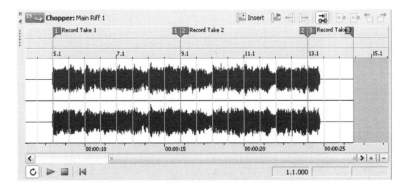

When using the Chopper, you can easily double-click on the waveform between regions to select the entire measure. Even better, you can also double-click and, on the second click, hold and drag to select subsequent regions.

The procedure for selecting measures is the same for Sound Forge.

You don't have to limit yourself just to one-shots. You can combine any track type together for a unique and creative twist.

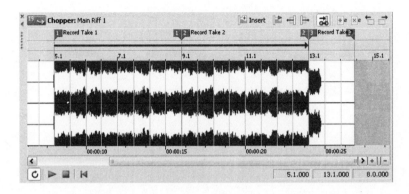

Constructing New Loops Using Different Events

You can also create new loops by arranging different types of events together on the same track or by combining events from different tracks. These events can be from just about any track type.

Using one-shot percussion tracks, for example, you can construct an entirely new percussion loop.

1. Open a few one-shots that would comprise a simple drum kit: a kick, a snare, a hi-hat, and a cymbal.

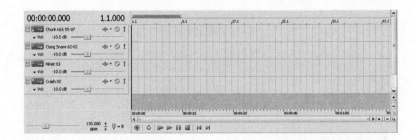

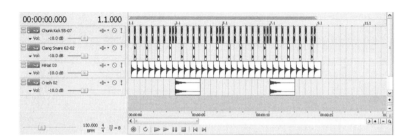

2. Paint in a desired rhythm for each track. An easy way to do this is by holding down Ctrl on your keyboard with the Paint Tool active. This will paint in the one-shots in their entirety.

You can set the grid resolution to a desired note value by right-clicking Marker Bar>Grid Spacing and choosing a desired value. You may also click the drop-down menu arrow to the right of the Enable Snapping button.

Once you construct your new rhythm, you can continue with the section, "Rendering to a New Loop."

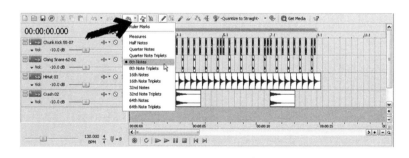

As mentioned, you don't have to limit yourself to just one-shots. Arrange events from loops in a similar manner. Use the standard copy and paste (or paste repeat) commands or use the Draw Tool to move around and arrange loop events.

It probably goes without saying that having some basic music theory skills will help you in creating the rhythm you have envisioned in your mind.

Insert Event at Play Cursor/ Paste Event At Play Cursor

You can also use the Insert Event at Play Cursor or Paste Event at Play Cursor commands to create an arrangement of events to be created as a loop later. These events can be of different types of tracks, from loops to one-shots to MIDI tracks.

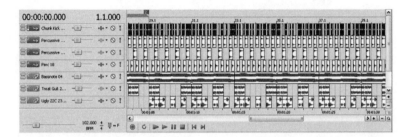

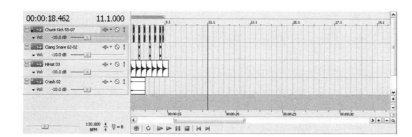

To insert an event at the play cursor:

1. Click on a track using the Draw Tool or the Selection Tool.

2. Place the play cursor in a desired location.

3. Start playback of your project.

4. Press Y on your keyboard. The selected track's entire event contents are inserted and snap to the nearest grid resolution.

5. Repeat as desired.

If you don't want to snap to the nearest set grid resolution, turn off snapping by pressing F8 on your keyboard.

You can set the Loop Region over a specific area and turn loop playback on (L on your keyboard) to help you concentrate on a specific part of your project.

To paste an event at the play cursor:

1. Click on a track using the Draw Tool or the Selection Tool.

Pasting an event is usually best when you want to insert only portions of an event such as a loop or MIDI event.

2. Copy an event or parts of an event to the clipboard by selecting the event and then using Ctrl+C.

3. Place the play cursor in a desired location.

4. Start playback of your project.

5. Press Shift+Y on your keyboard. The contents of the clipboard will be inserted and snap to the nearest grid resolution (if snapping is on).

6. Repeat as desired.

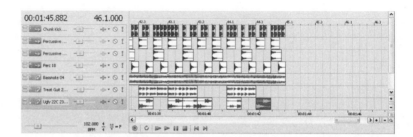

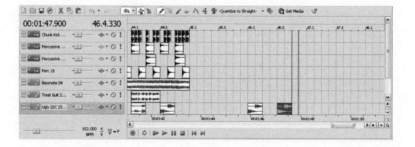

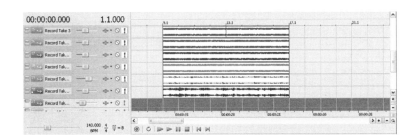

MIDI Tracks

A MIDI track's events are composed or constructed the same way just like any other digital audio event, but if you expect to bounce them down to a new track as digital audio, they must be routed to a DLS, VST instrument or ReWire soft synth.

Rendering a New Loop

Watching dB Levels

When rendering to a new track (also called, "bouncing down") to create a new loop, you should solo the track (or tracks) involved and mix them as close to unity (0.0 dBFS) as possible without clipping.

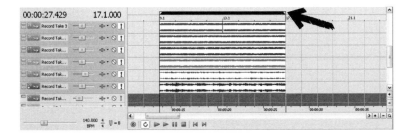

To render a track to a new track:

1. Solo the track by clicking the track and pressing X on your keyboard.

2. Click and drag the Loop Region over the area you'd like to bounce down in the Marker Bar.

3. Turn loop playback on (L or Q on your keyboard) to concentrate on that specific part of the project. Begin playback of your project.

4. Watch the Master meter in the Mixer during playback. Mix the levels of your tracks so that they get close to unity without clipping. Stop playback once satisfied

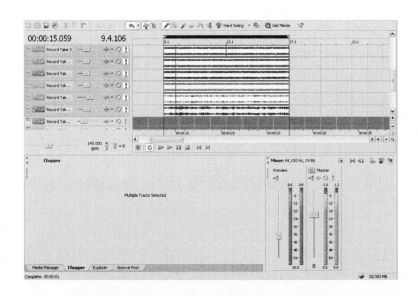

You can keep or delete the original tracks in your project if you'd like. Remember to mute them so they don't interfere with your newly rendered track.

5. Press Ctrl+M to render the audio to a new track. Be sure to check the "render loop region only" option. Give your track a new name and click Save. The new track will then be added to your project. You can then mix this new track with the rest of your project.

A newly rendered track's individual track volume will be set according to the Preview meter's fader setting in the Mixer. Don't be alarmed if the newly rendered track's volume sounds lower than the original. Just set the track volume accordingly.

The newly rendered track will also be ACIDized based on the length of the audio. See the section "ACIDized Track Types" later in this chapter for more information.

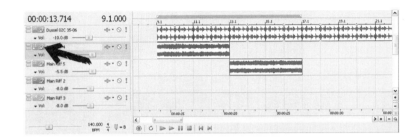

Stretch Markers, Beat Markers, and Beat Anchors

Once the audio is bounced down, you'll probably want to customize the stretching properties of the track to optimize its sound quality when it stretches to other tempos.

Ideally, you'll want to add stretch markers to accent any subdivision of a beat you feel needs stressing.

To customize stretching properties for a track:

1. Double-click the track's icon in the track list.

2. Click the Stretch tab.

3. Add a stretch marker by double-clicking the marker bar at the bottom underneath the waveform.

You can disable snapping by pressing F8 on your keyboard or holding down Shift while dragging to perform more precise marker placement.

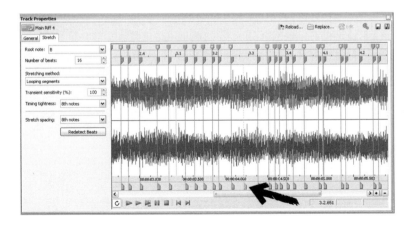

You can (and probably should) save the ACIDized properties to the track itself once you're done adding, subtracting and adjusting stretch markers. Click the Save or Save As buttons to do so.

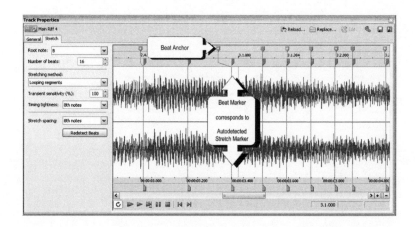

The Save button will destroy and replace the original track you presently have in your project, while the Save As button will replace the original track under a new name and leave the original track alone.

Beat anchors, beat markers, and autodetected stretch markers are different in that they override the present groove or rhythm when quantized. They do not affect the way your loop sounds if you were to paint them on the Timeline normally. Beat anchors and beat/stretch markers come into play when using the Groove Tool and the "Quantize to Straight" groove. See chapter 7 for more information on grooves and the Groove Tool.

By adjusting the beat anchor, the beat marker, or the autodetected stretch marker, the audio present at the beat marker/autodetected stretch marker will be played at the corresponding beat anchor, essentially "warping" the sound.

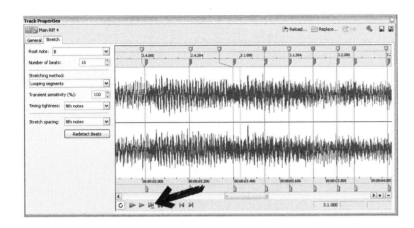

Any autodetected stretch marker always has a corresponding beat marker right below the beat ruler and a line drawing to the beat anchor it corresponds to.

Use the Play Quantized button to hear how the groove changes your existing audio.

Once you adjust the groove to your liking, you can use the Add to Groove Pool button to add the groove to the Groove Pool for further editing and tweaking.

Be sure that if your bounced audio does not have a definite pitch, like percussion tracks, set your project's key to None. Set it back to the original key after bouncing.

ACIDization of Rendered Loops

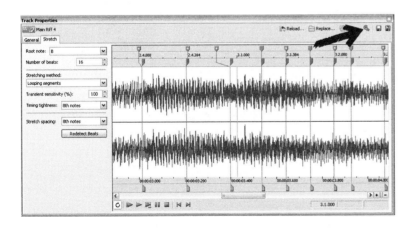

When you render audio to a new track, the newly rendered, bounced-down track is automatically ACIDized to include tempo and key info (if applicable) of the active project. For example, if your project is set at a tempo of 140bpm in the key of C, so will your newly rendered track be ACIDized for a tempo of 140bpm in the key of C.

ACIDized Track Types

The length of the rendered audio will determine exactly what kind of ACIDized track the audio will become.

You can tell the track type by looking at its icon in the track list:

- **Loop:** The most common track. Anything rendered between half a second to 30 seconds becomes a loop.

- **Beatmapped:** Anything rendered that's longer than 30 seconds becomes a beatmapped track.

- **One-shot:** Anything shorter than half a second becomes a one-shot. This format is ideal for percussive hits and spoken dialog material.

You can adjust the default settings to determine what kind of track the rendered audio becomes by going to the Audio tab under Options>Preferences on the menu bar and adjusting the "Open as loops if between (seconds)" setting. Anything between the two settings is seen as a loop. Anything shorter is seen as a one-shot, and anything longer is seen as a beatmapped track.

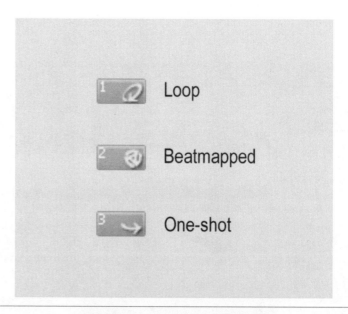

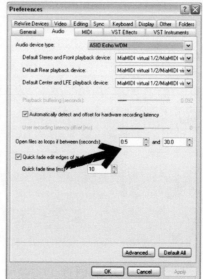

Chapter 10

Recording Audio

One way to make yourself stand out from the crowd is to create your own original material. Most of the time that involves recording your own content, whether it be MIDI or digital audio. This chapter will discuss in some detail on how to go about doing the latter.

Audio Recording Hardware

It probably goes without saying that if you want professional-quality audio, you'll need to invest in good hardware. The latest game cards may sound good, but they really can't compare with the performance and support of the pro-level interfaces like those from Echo or M-Audio—companies that specialize in audio interfaces for digital audio workstations.

There are lots of choices, from internal PCI offerings to external USB (1.1 and 2.0) and FireWire interfaces. There are also external choices that interface with a PCI card. Depending on what you want, these choices may be affordable, especially if you work solo. Echo's MiaMIDI and M-Audio's Audiophile 2496 are great cards to start with.

Be sure to use quality cables for good signal transfer. Also ensure that the instrument being used has its output volume set as loud as possible without clipping.

If you're looking for an external interface that's mobile, go for either USB 2.0 or FireWire. High-quality audio can be too much for USB 1.1's much narrower bandwidth.

When recording via S/PDIF, which is a digital format, you must slave your audio interface to the recording source in order for accurate bit-for-bit digital transfer to occur. Again, be sure to consult your audio interface's manual as well as your recording source's manual on how to set both up to record via S/PDIF.

Setting Audio Device Preferences

By default, ACID Pro is set to use Microsoft Sound Mapper as its playback device, but you'll almost always want to change this option, since choosing a different driver model (that is, one that was specifically written for the audio device you're using) will allow you to choose a specific input for recording. The two most important driver models are below.

ASIO

ASIO is a driver model developed by Steinberg that lets the audio application you're using (in this case, ACID) talk directly to the hardware. It's the best choice for recording MIDI but can also definitely be used to record digital audio.

The downside to ASIO is that you're allowed to physically use only one audio interface in your system at a time.

Windows Classic Wave

Generally, a couple of different driver models fall under this category, the most popular nowadays being Windows Driver Model. Some vendors have their own version of a driver model, like Echo's PureWave, which bypasses the Windows Kmixer and lets the hardware and application talk directly to each other for better-sounding audio. This means the Echo devices have a more robust sound.

The downside to Windows Classic Wave is that it's not ideal for MIDI. However it's more flexible than ASIO in terms of letting you use multiple audio interfaces for playback, routing, and recording.

When recording S/PDIF via RCA coaxial, you must use a cable that has 75Ohms resistance, as it's the standard for S/PDIF. Otherwise, you might end up with garbage or even no audio at all. If you need an RCA S/PDIF cable in a pinch, you can use a standard RCA video cable (color-coded yellow plugs), as they're rated at that resistance.

To change the audio device for play-back:

1. Select Options>Preferences on ACID's menu bar.

2. Click the Audio tab.

3. Under Audio device type, choose a specific driver model from the drop-down list. As soon as you choose a driver model, available outputs for playback should be available immediately underneath.

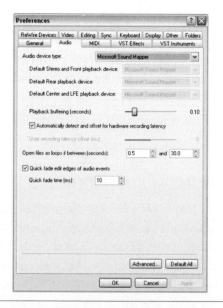

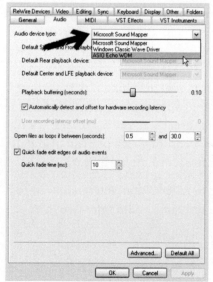

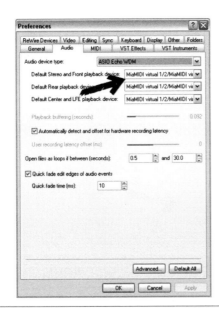

4. Choose a stereo and front device for main playback. Choose a rear, center and LFE device for surround playback. (Note that you must have separate physical outputs for each listed channel for surround to work properly.)

ACID is not capable of recording multiple tracks simultaneously.

5. If you choose ASIO as your driver model, you should have the Advanced button available. Clicking this button will bring up a dialog with driver name, buffer settings, and clock source (sample rate).

Clicking the Configure button will bring up your audio interface's buffer settings so you can adjust ASIO latency. Note that each audio interface's ASIO buffer settings and interfaces are different.

Once you're done here, click your way back to the main ACID window by clicking OK. You are now ready to begin recording.

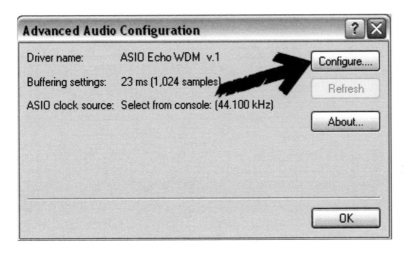

The Record Window

To record:

1. Click the Record button in the transport toolbar, or press Ctrl+R on your keyboard.

2. Set your parameters and click the Record button in the Record window. Record your material.

3. When recording, the Record button in the Record window will turn into a Stop button. Click this button to stop your recording and add the recording to your project.

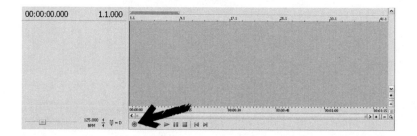

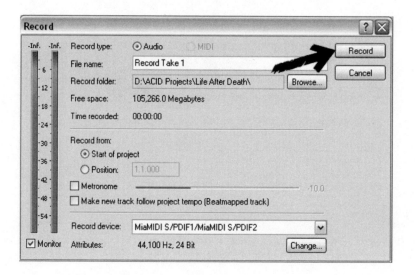

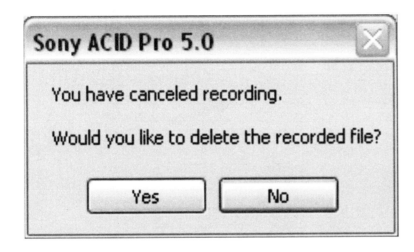

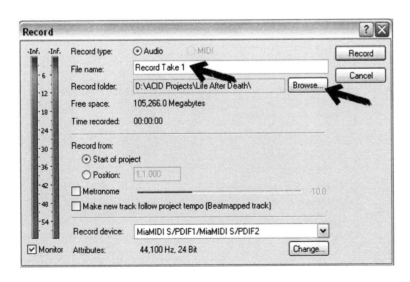

If you don't like the take as you're recording, you can press the Cancel button underneath the Stop button. ACID will confirm that you canceled recording and ask if you'd like to delete the recording. Click Yes to keep the recording (which will add the recording to the project) or No to delete the recording.

When you first launch the Record window, you'll notice that you have a few options available to you.

By default, any new recording is labeled, Record Take X (where X is a number). You can rename the take to anything you'd like.

You can also browse to a folder where you want to save the recording by clicking the Browse button.

You can set any and all recordings to default to your current project's location (such as the same folder the project is in) by setting either the "single default folder" or "separate defaults for each type" to <Project>. As long as you first save the project in a specific location, the recordings will follow suit and be saved in the same location.

You can choose a position to start recording from, either from the start of the project or a specific location (in measures:beats:ticks). You can place the cursor anywhere, but I'd recommend at least a couple of measures just to give yourself breathing room.

If you don't plan to stretch your take to other tempos and just want to record the audio as is, you can uncheck the option "Make new track follow project tempo (Beatmapped track)." This will effectively turn your recording into a one-shot, the only ACIDized form of audio that ACID does not stretch.

Placing the cursor before opening the Record window will automatically set the record start position to be at the cursor position.

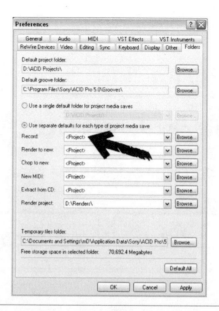

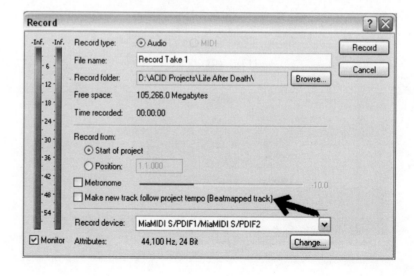

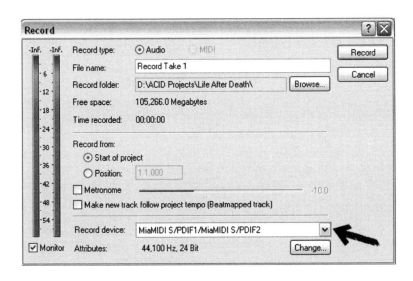

Choose a specific hardware input for recording under "Record device." This will ensure that only the specific input is recorded and not your entire project as it plays back.

I'd suggest leaving the Monitor meter on so you can at least check the levels of your incoming signal, especially when recording digitally, so that your recording doesn't clip.

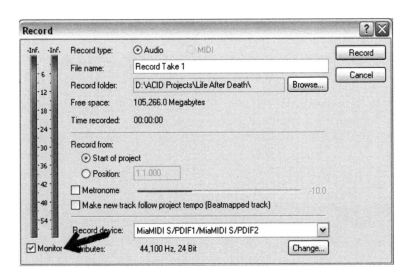

You can change the bit-depth and sample rate settings for the recording by clicking the Change button. Note that this will also change your overall project's bit depth and sample rate as well.

Because of the limitations of USB 1.1 audio, you may not be able to monitor your input while playing back. Be sure to read your audio interface's documentation fully.

Monitoring While Recording via Hardware

You'll probably want to monitor your input signal while playing back, recording or just letting your application sit idle while you listen to the input. Just about all pro-level audio hardware should allow you to do this.

Some interfaces do this for you automatically. Some need a little more configuring in order to monitor while playing back. You would have to go into the audio interface's software and unmute the appropriate input and turn its sliders all the way up. Check your interface's documentation to find out how to do this.

Remember that ACID cannot do input monitoring itself. It must be done via the audio hardware.

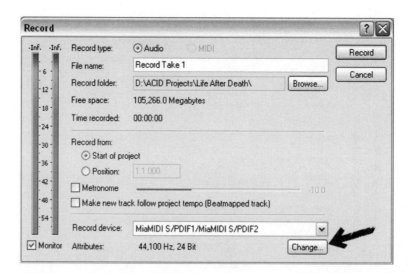

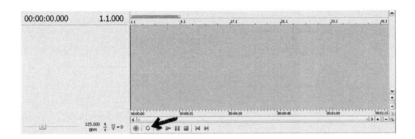

Recording Multiple Takes

You can record multiple takes by turning loop playback on (L or Q on your keyboard), setting the Loop Region over the area you want to concentrate on and record to your heart's content.

To record multiple takes:

1. Turn Loop Playback on by pressing the Loop Playback button on the transport toolbar or by pressing L or Q on your keyboard.

2. Set the Loop Region over the area you'd like to loop.

3. Record as usual.

ACID will keep looping the same area of your project over and over again but will record your take as one long track. You can then decide what you want to do with the track after you record.

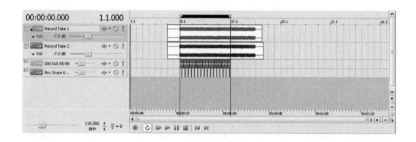

Recorded takes have regions automatically applied to them for each measure in the recorded track's properties and the Chopper. This makes it much easier to glean what you want from the take, especially when using the Chopper. For more information, see Chapter 9, "Chopping to a New Track Using the Chopper."

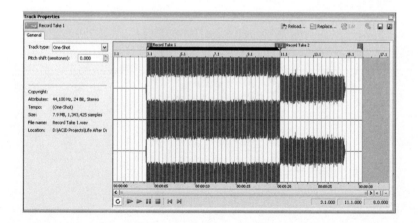

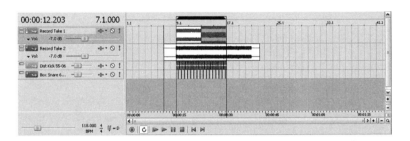

Working with Recorded Tracks

You can work with recorded tracks like you can any other track in ACID, including applying effects and routing. You can chop, draw, erase, paint, bounce down, or perform any other function relating to audio events.

To trim recorded tracks:

1. Click the Draw Tool button in ACID's main toolbar.

You'll probably want to trim the beginning and end of recorded events, as they'll usually contain audio you may not want to hear, like string squeaks while preparing to play guitar. Don't worry; the audio data remains but will not play back.

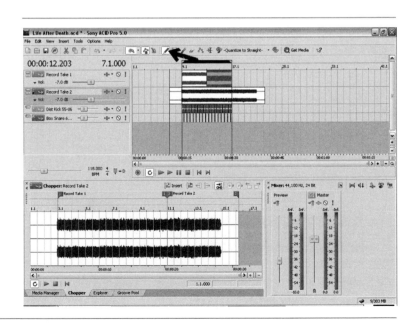

2. Hover the cursor over the edge of the track's event until you see the pointer change into the event edge cursor, then click and drag to trim the audio.

To temporarily override snapping, hold down Shift on your keyboard after you start clicking and dragging.

If snapping is on, the edge will snap to the nearest grid resolution. You can temporarily override this by holding down Shift on your keyboard while clicking and dragging. Remember to click and drag first before holding down Shift.

You can also trim the recorded track's event by using the Time Selection Tool:

1. Click the track's event so that only the event is selected.

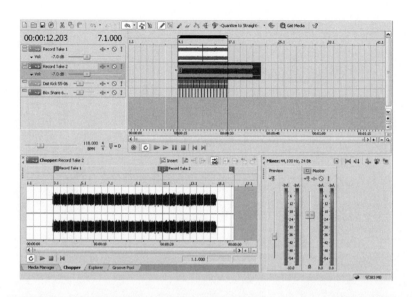

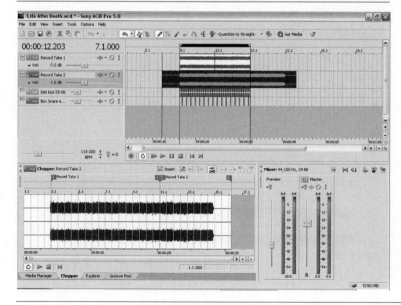

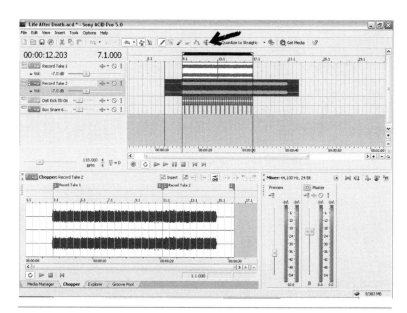

2. Click the Time Selection Tool button.

3. Click and drag the Loop Region over the area that you'd like to keep, then press Ctrl+T on your keyboard. The event is now trimmed.

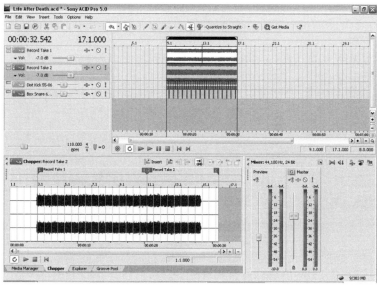

Using the Metronome

The metronome is a new, much wished-for feature that you can use to follow a project's tempo while recording. You can enable the metronome by either pressing the Metronome button in ACID's main toolbar or by enabling the Metronome option under the Record dialog and setting the slider to a desired volume.

Use the Preview fader to adjust the metronome's volume when not using the Record window.

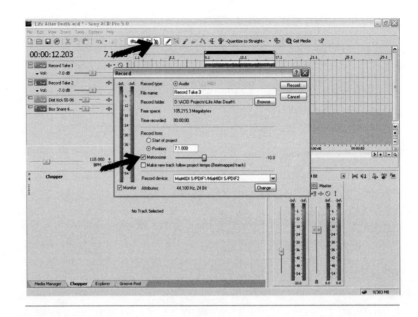

Chapter 11

Recording MIDI

The Musical Instrument Digital Interface (MIDI) standard was introduced in January 1983 as a way of controlling electronic keyboards and sound modules remotely from another keyboard or computer. It is very similar in concept to the player piano that was invented almost a hundred years earlier in 1890. Using a series of Note On and Note Off events, much like the holes in a player piano roll, you can record the keyboard actions and store them to be played back later on any MIDI-enabled device.

The advantage of recording MIDI loops in ACID is that they transpose and stretch with absolutely no artifacts because the transposition and stretching is done by generating notes in a new key or generating Note On and Note Off events at a slower or faster tempo. Best of all, you can easily turn MIDI loops into audio loops by rendering them.

You might use ACID and never record your own loops, but if you play an instrument that is MIDI-enabled, you'll probably want to add your own loops to your composition. Recording loops or even entire tracks ensures the uniqueness of the composition and adds a personal touch that no one else will have. ACID supports instrument plug-ins that conform to Virtual Studio Technology (VST) instruments interface introduced by Steinberg. It comes with a DLS soft synth, and ACID Pro 5.0 includes Native Instruments Keyboard Express. VST instruments give you a virtual recording studio full of instruments right in your computer. VST instrument manufacturers have recreated some of the classic keyboard instruments at a fraction of the price

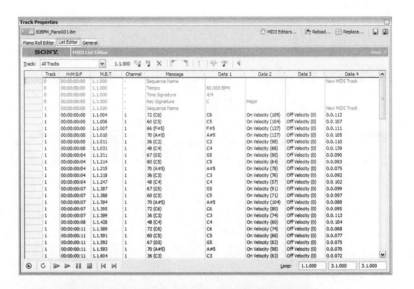

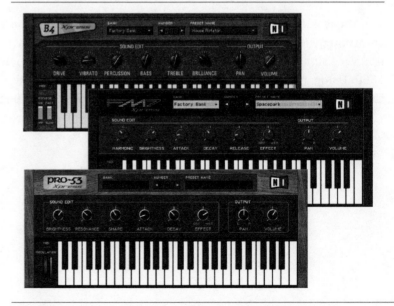

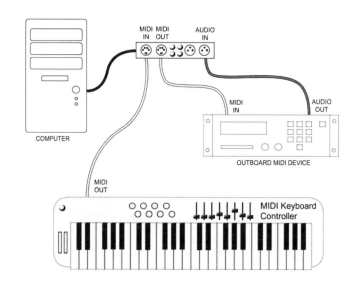

of their original hardware counterparts. Likewise, VST instrument samplers bring entire orchestras to your fingertips.

MIDI Recording Hardware

There are two ways to record MIDI data into ACID. One way is to insert an empty MIDI track and use the Piano Roll Editor to enter the notes manually. Using this technique, you do not need any MIDI hardware. If, however, you want to record your MIDI performance from a real piano keyboard or other MIDI controller, you will need to set up your hardware properly. There are three hardware devices needed to record MIDI:

- A MIDI input device such as a MIDI keyboard controller or other MIDI instrument.

- A MIDI interface to plug your keyboard controller into.

- A MIDI output device such as soft synths, a sound card, or outboard MIDI modules.

Selecting a MIDI Controller

Selecting the right MIDI input device could be a challenge. If you are a keyboard player—you play piano, organ, synthesizer, or other keyboard instrument—you will want to have a controller with at least 49 keys. This provides four octaves, which should be enough to use both hands when needed. Acoustic pianos have 88 notes. If you are a serious pianist, you might consider an 88-note MIDI controller with weighted keys to get as close as you can to a real piano feel.

If you do not play a keyboard instrument or you just want to play solo parts like bass, horns, and chord pads, you might consider one of the 25-note MIDI keyboard controllers. Since they are about the same size as a laptop computer, they have the advantage of being small and portable so you can take them on the road and use them in a hotel room with relative ease.

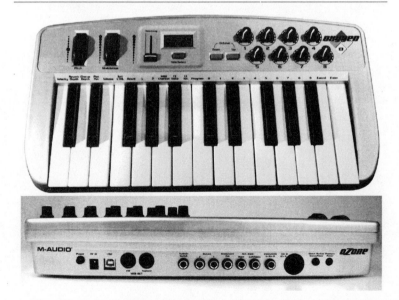

Another thing to consider is whether you plan to use VST instruments and control their parameters from your keyboard. Many MIDI keyboard controllers come with a selection of knobs and sliders that can send MIDI control data to anther device. This control data will allow you to manipulate the virtual knobs and sliders on your VST instrument from your hardware controller.

Selecting a MIDI Interface

A MIDI interface is required to plug the MIDI keyboard into your computer. There are three ways to accomplish this:

1. Use a internal sound card that has MIDI input jacks that accept MIDI cables from your MIDI keyboard controller.

2. Use an external USB or FireWire device that provides outboard MIDI input jacks that accept MIDI cables from your MIDI keyboard controller.

3. Use a USB MIDI keyboard that plugs into the USB port on your computer. These keyboards actually have an internal USB-to-MIDI converter and may even have extra external MIDI jacks to plug other controllers or MIDI sound modules into.

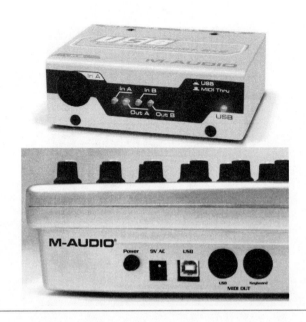

If you already have a MIDI keyboard, the first and second options will allow you to plug it into your computer with your existing MIDI cables. I have an external USB-to-MIDI converter for use with my laptop computer. However you decide to interface your MIDI controller with your computer, one of these methods will meet your needs.

Selecting a MIDI Output Device

The final hardware consideration is your MIDI output device. This can be an internal soundcard or an external USB or FireWire device. Since MIDI data is very low-bandwidth, it does not matter which you use for monitoring your MIDI recording. At some point, however, you are going to want to render your MIDI as audio so it can be burned to a CD or other final format. At that point, I would recommend a

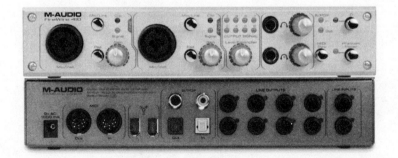

professional soundcard, or even better, an external FireWire or PCI audio device. Outboard devices are impervious to computer noise from hard drives since they are outside the case. USB 1.1 is not a good option for audio because of its limited bandwidth.

If you are using outboard MIDI sound modules as instruments, their MIDI inputs must connect to the MIDI output jacks on your computer and MIDI interface. During your final mix, you will need to route their audio outputs back into your computer as audio inputs. See the Recording Audio chapter on how to accomplish this. If you are using VST instruments, ACID will render the output into the final mix automatically. This is the easiest option to use.

Plugging It All Together

Once you have selected all of your components, you are ready to plug them together. Your MIDI controller may have several MIDI ports. There are three types of MIDI ports.

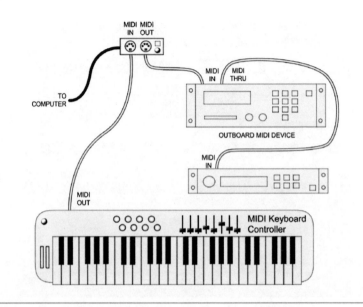

1. **MIDI IN:** This port accepts MIDI data into the MIDI keyboard. This is usually found only on MIDI keyboards that have internal sound-generation capabilities so that they can be controlled from another MIDI keyboard or computer. If you want to use your MIDI keyboard as a sound source, connect the MIDI OUT port of your computer to this MIDI IN port.

2. **MIDI OUT:** This port sends MIDI data from the keyboard to another device. This is the port that connects to the MIDI IN port of your computer.

3. **MIDI THRU:** This port will echo any MIDI data coming in from the MIDI IN port. It allows a pass-through of MIDI data so that devices can be daisy-chained together.

EFFECTS TECHNOLOGY

INSTRUMENT TECHNOLOGY

Note: ACID does not support DXi instruments

If you are planning on using an external MIDI device for sounds, you will need to route the audio output of those devices into the audio input of your sound card. See Chapter 10, Recording Audio, which explains how to accomplish this.

When purchasing virtual MIDI instruments for use in ACID, make sure they are VST-instrument compatible. ACID does not support DXi instruments.

VST Instrument Setup

Steinberg introduced the original Virtual Studio Technology (VST) as a way of plugging effects into host recording software. Steinberg expanded this technology to include virtual instruments and called them VST instruments. Microsoft introduced their effect plug-in technology as part of DirectX. Their virtual instrument technology is called DXi. ACID supports VST instruments but not DXi instruments. ACID also supports DirectX effect plug-ins. And as of version 5, it supports VST effect plug-ins as well. This is important to know. When you purchase instrument plug-ins, make sure they are VST-instrument compatible.

There are many manufacturers of VST instruments. Arturia makes classic synths like the Moog Modular, Minimoog, CS-80, and ARP 2600. Native Instruments has emulations of classic keyboards like the Hammond B3, Prophet 5, Yamaha DX 7, and Rhodes/Wurlitzer. You probably couldn't afford to buy the hardware counterparts of these soft synths even if you could find one in working condition. Purchasing these emulated versions is a great way to own the classic keyboards of the past.

There are also many free VST instruments on the Internet, and some of them are very high -quality. A good resource for these is www.kvraudio.com.

ACID refers to VST instruments as soft synths. The first step to being ready to record MIDI is to set your MIDI input device in the preferences.

To set up your MIDI input and output device:

1. Select Options>Preferences.

2. Click the MIDI tab.

3. From the top list (MIDI output devices), select any MIDI output device you want to use, like your soundcard or outboard MIDI gear. If you are just using VST instruments, you can leave this selection blank.

4. From the bottom list (MIDI input devices), select the MIDI input port that your MIDI keyboard controller is plugged into, or if you are using a USB controller, you can select the controller itself.

5. Click OK.

Next, you should tell ACID where you have your virtual instruments installed. By default ACID will look in the C:\Program Files\VSTplugins\directory. This is a good place to install your virtual instruments.

To tell ACID where else to search:

1. Select Options>Preferences.

2. Click the VST Instruments tab.

Keep your VST instruments and VST effects in separate folders on your hard drive.

3. Next to "Alternate VSTi search folder 1" or "Alternate VSTi search folder 2," type the full path name or click the Browse button to find the folder. This will tell ACID where else to look for VST instruments.

4. Click OK.

I recommend that you install your instruments into the default location to make things simpler. Some instruments incorrectly report that they are also effects when, in fact, they are not. I recommend that you keep your VST instruments in a separate folder from your VST effects to eliminate this problem.

To insert a VST instrument:

1. Select Insert>Soft Synth from the main menu or click the Insert Soft Synth button above the bus area.

2. Select a soft synth from the Soft Synth Chooser dialog. ACID Pro 4.0 comes with one soft synth by default, called Sony DLS Soft Synth. If you have not installed any soft synths, this will be the only one in the list. ACID Pro 5 also includes NI Keyboard Express VSTi soft synths.

3. Click OK.

You should now see the Soft Synth Properties dialog, which will allow you to control the soft synth. The first thing you will want to do is select the sound or instrument that you want the soft synth to use. This will vary depending on which soft synth you loaded. If you use the Sony DLS Soft Synth, there will be a list of instruments to choose from. For some soft synths like samplers or Soundfont players, you will need to load a file with the sound in it. You can also set the MIDI channel that you want this soft synth to respond to. There are 16 MIDI channels, so you can have your tracks routed to 16 different MIDI soft synths.

Multi-Port VST Instruments

Some VSTi soft synths have multiple outputs. ACID Pro 5.0 will create a soft synth bus for every output the instrument exposes. When assigning a multi-port soft synth to a track you will notice that there is only one soft synth listed in the track assignment drop-down list. The reason is that it is still just one multi-timbre instrument. You can assign this instrument to two

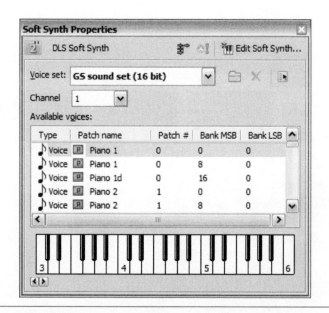

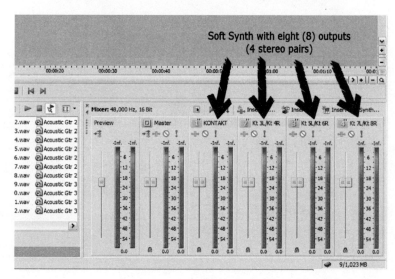

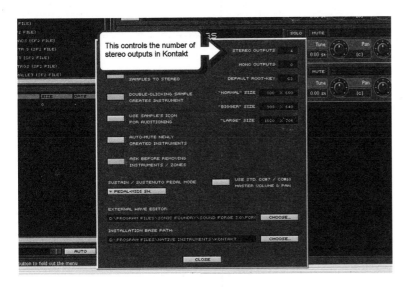

(or more) tracks in ACID. Have one track set to a different MIDI channel. Then in your instrument, have it respond to that MIDI channel on separate output with different sounds (patches) assigned to it.

For example, Kontakt can have up to 32 outputs (16 stereo pairs). You can load several different samples into Kontakt, have it listen to a different MIDI channel to trigger each sample, and have it route each sample to a different stereo output. This allows you to control the volumes in ACID via the extra soft synth buses. Previously, you would have to mix these sounds in Kontakt itself. The multi-port output also allows you to add FX to each output separately. Kontakt has preferences that tell ACID how many outputs to create (1-16 stereo pairs). This capability isn't found in every VSTi.

Making Your MIDI Recording

Before you start to record, there is one customization I recommend you make. Because MIDI is a series of Note On and Note Off messages, it is very easy to stop playback after a Note On message is sent but before a Note Off message is sent. This results in stuck notes or notes that play forever. Luckily, ACID has a quick fix for this. There is a menu item under Tools>Reset All MIDI Ports. Unfortunately, when a MIDI note is blasting in your ear, the last thing you have time to do is fumble through the menus looking for that option. Fortunately, ACID's toolbar is customizable, so you can add this as a button to the toolbar, where it can be easily accessed.

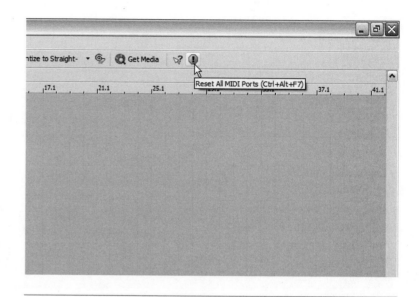

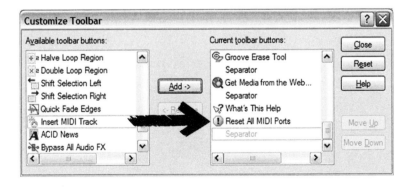

To add the Reset All MIDI Ports Button
to the toolbar:

1. Double-click the left mouse button
   anywhere on the blank area of the
   toolbar.

2. From the Customize Toolbar dialog,
   scroll down the left list of available
   toolbar buttons until you come to
   Reset All MIDI Ports and highlight
   it.

3. Click the Add-> button to add it to
   the end of the Current toolbar buttons list.

4. Click the Close button.

**Place the All
MIDI-off button
on the toolbar.**

You should now have the Reset All
MIDI Ports button at the end of your
toolbar, where you can get to it quickly
when you need it.

Before you start to record, it is a good
idea to set the file folders to store your
recorded tracks where you want them.

To set your properties so that ACID keeps all files pertaining to a single project in the same directory use:

Keep each project in a separate directory with all its files. Be sure to save the project at least once to establish the project folder location.

1. Select Options>Preferences.

2. Click the Folders tab.

3. Select the radio button "Use a single default folder for project media save."

4. Select <Project> as the default folder.

5. Click OK.

ACID will now use the project folder to store all its files, making it easier to keep track of which files go with each project. Alternately, you can have ACID store each type of project media in a separate folder.

Once you have made this change, it is a good idea to save your project at least once before recording. This will establish the default project folder. The next time you press the Record button, ACID will already have the project folder selected as the target for all your MIDI files.

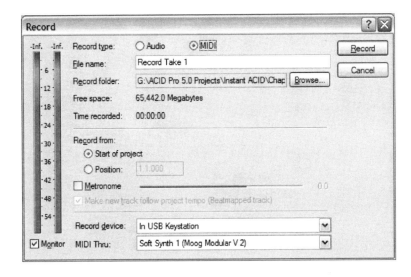

When you are ready to record:

1. Press the red Record button or Ctrl+R to bring up the record dialog.

2. Make sure MIDI is the selected under "Record type" at the top of the dialog box.

3. In the File name field, give your recording a meaningful name. This name is also used on the scribble strip of the track. ACID will not allow you to record over an existing file and will prompt you for a new name if the one you've chosen already exists.

4. Select whether to begin recording from the start of the project or from the current cursor location.

The Record folder is the location that the recorded files will be stored in. It is a good idea to start each project in its work subdirectory so that all the recorded files are kept in one place. You will probably have a lot of the same names (for example, kick, snare, bass, and lead guitar) for your recorded tracks in other songs, so getting into the habit of using a new directory for each new project keeps file names in order.

Using the Metronome

ACID Pro 5 has a metronome for keeping time. Just like its real-world counterpart, the metronome in ACID will click in time to the project tempo as a tempo reference while you record.

The metronome is a new feature in ACID 5 to help you keep time while recording.

Check the Metronome checkbox in the Record dialog box to enable the metronome and set its volume.

You can set the metronome volume from –Infinity to +12dB. The volume is changeable during recording, so you might want to click Record, adjust the metronome volume, then click Cancel and select Yes to delete the recorded file. This is an easy way to set the metronome volume.

If you have an earlier version of ACID, it is best to add a drum track before the first recording to help keep time. It does not have to be the final drums for the song. It's just a scratch track that could be replaced later.

Record from:
- Start of project
- Position: 1.1.000
- ☑ Metronome ————————☐———— 0.0
- ☑ Make new track follow project tempo (Beatmapped track)

Record device: In USB Keystation

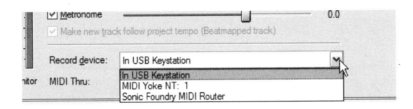

Selecting the Recording Device

At the bottom of the Record dialog are the "Record device" and "MIDI Thru."

1. Make sure that the Record device is set to the MIDI controller or MIDI input on your computer.

2. MIDI Thru should be set to the soft synth or external MIDI device that you want to use to monitor your recording. This device is automatically assigned to the recorded track.

Monitor works differently for MIDI tracks than it does for audio tracks. Checking the Monitor checkbox enables the viewing of MIDI velocity on the VU meters and not the actual audio output of the Soft Synth. Even when it is unchecked, you can still hear the MIDI device playing.

Once all the settings are correct you should only need to change the take name for subsequent recordings.

Recording

Before recording, it is best to determine if a count-in is required to help align playing with the tempo of the song. This is only needed if your song requires the MIDI track to start playing on the first beat of the song. Since ACID doesn't have a count-in or pre-roll function, place a one measure count on a separate track and start all of your loop painting at the first beat of the second measure of the Timeline.

Press the Record button to start recording. If the metronome is enabled, you should hear it click in time to the tempo. The Time at Cursor and Measure and Beat Cursor readouts will display the time and beat locations respectively. Record the part and click the Stop button when recording is complete.

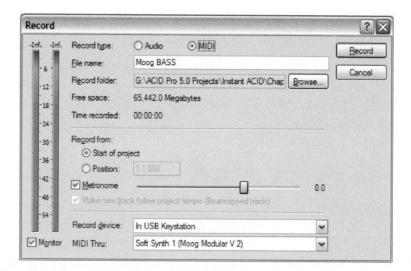

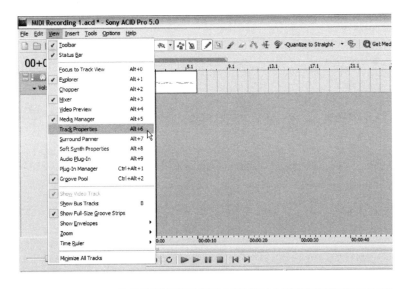

Working with Track Properties

There are four ways to open the Track Properties that will be used interchangeably throughout the remainder of this chapter. It is important to note that any one of these techniques will get you to the same place.

To open the Track Properties after you have highlighted the track

- Select View>Track Properties from the main menu.

- Press Alt+6.

- Double-click the track number in the track header.

- Right-click the track header and select Properties.

Whenever an instruction says to open the track properties, you can use any one of these techniques.

Heads and Tails and What To Do About Them

If you are recording a loop, and the loop started on the first beat, you probably have a measure of silence before your loop because you had to wait a measure to sync with the tempo. You may also have some amount of silence at the end that you need to remove. These unwanted heads and tails can be removed with the Piano Roll Editor.

To remove silence at the start of a MIDI loop:

1. Open the Track Properties by highlighting the track and pressing Alt+6.

2. In the Track Properties select the Piano Roll Editor tab.

3. Press Ctrl+A to select all of the MIDI events.

4. Left-click on the first event and drag it to the first beat, making sure you stay on the same note.

5. Click the Save File icon to save the new location of the events in the MIDI file.

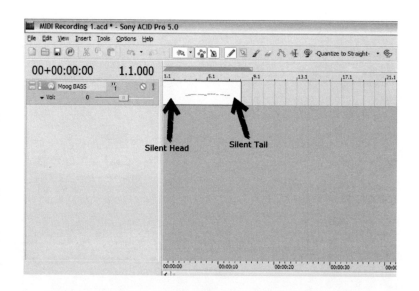

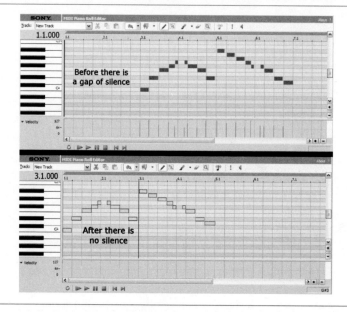

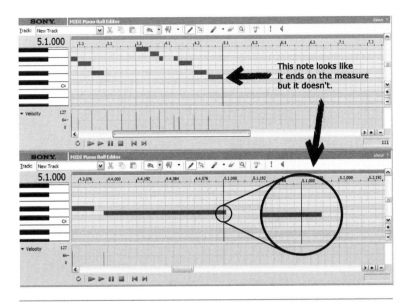

This note looks like it ends on the measure but it doesn't.

MIDI notes that extend just slightly past the end of the measure cause unwanted silent tails at the end of a MIDI loop. This causes ACID to extend the MIDI loop duration for an additional measure. When you try looping the event, there will be a measure of silence at the end of the loop.

To remove silence at the end of a MIDI loop:

1. Open the Track properties by highlighting the track and pressing Alt+6.

2. In the Track Properties, select the Piano Roll Editor tab.

3. Scroll to the right of the MIDI notes and look for notes that extend slightly beyond the boundary of the last measure.

4. Use the Draw Tool (Ctrl+D) to shorten all the notes that extend beyond the last measure boundary.

Strategy for Recording MIDI Loops

I find that when recording MIDI loops it's important for the loop to flow naturally. Most musicians play the first measure differently from subsequent measures. There is something about anticipating the first beat of the first measure that makes you play a little harder or a little stiffer than you do on the first beat of the second measure. For these reasons, I like to record several measures of a loop and then select the best performance from those measures to be the final loop. I find that this produces a more natural-sounding loop.

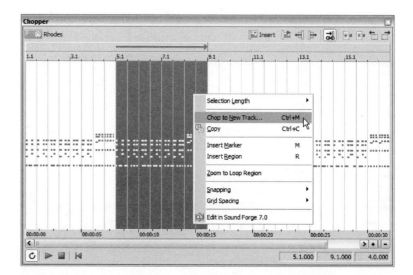

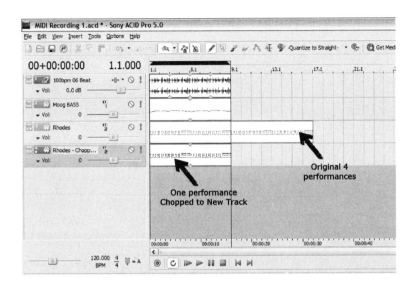

One performance
Chopped to New Track

Original 4
performances

To select the best performance from a recording:

1. Right-click on the loop and choose Select in Chopper.

2. Audition each measure in the chopper until you find one that has a nice looping groove. Use the < and > keys to move the selection left and right while auditioning.

3. Right-click on the selection you like best and choose Chop to New Track.

4. Give the loop a new name and click OK.

5. Right-click on an empty part of the original track and select Delete Track to remove it from the project.

You now have a new loop that is your best performance.

Tracks and MIDI Channels

ACID does not assign MIDI channels to tracks. This is because ACID allows you to place both formats of Standard MIDI Files (Format 0 and 1) files on a track. Standard MIDI Format 1 (SMF1) files can contain multiple MIDI tracks on multiple MIDI channels. This allows you to bring an entire song containing multiple channels in Standard MIDI Format into a single track in ACID. If you are recording your own MIDI tracks using soft synths, it is acceptable to keep everything on MIDI channel 1 because ACID assigns a single soft synth to a track, and it will only send MIDI information from that track to the soft synth. If you are using an external MIDI Device, you will have to assign the MIDI channel to the MIDI data within the track so that it corresponds to the MIDI channel the external MIDI device is listening to.

If you have a soft synth that can accept multiple MIDI channels, you can assign it to multiple ACID tracks and then assign the MIDI data in each track to play on a different channel. In this way you can drive a single soft synth from multiple ACID tracks. See Ad-

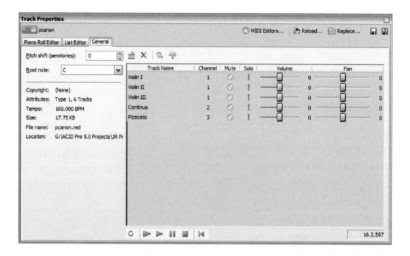

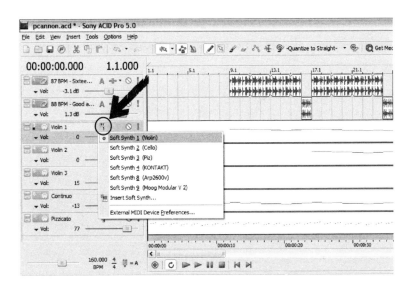

dressing Multi-Channel MIDI Devices in this chapter for steps on how to do this.

Routing to MIDI Devices

Each ACID track containing MIDI data has an icon of a MIDI jack next to the track number. Just to the right of the track name is a small keyboard with a number under it. This button controls the device routing for that track. Clicking the button opens the Context menu, which contains the MIDI devices you have defined in your preferences along with any soft synths you may have inserted. It will also give you the option of inserting a new soft synth or editing your external device preferences to add or remove a device.

You can use this menu to route an ACID track to any MIDI device you have. The number of the device from the menu will show beneath the icon in the track header. If you hover your mouse over the icon, the tool tip text will show the device name.

Addressing Multi-Channel MIDI Devices

If you have a VST instrument or external MIDI sound device that can load multiple sounds on multiple channels, you can assign that device to several ACID tracks and then assign a different MIDI channel with that track to trigger different instruments.

To change MIDI channel assignments in the Track Properties:

1. Open the Track Properties by highlighting the track and pressing Alt+6.

2. Select the General tab. This will show you all the MIDI tracks within the ACID track.

3. Double-click on in the Channel column for the track you want to change and type in the new MIDI channel.

The MIDI track will now drive any device assigned to the track that is listening on that MIDI channel. If your VST instrument soft synth supports multiple outputs, ACID will add a soft synth bus for each output. See Multi-Post VST Instruments in this chapter for more information.

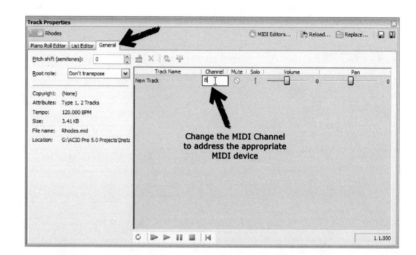

Change the MIDI Channel to address the appropriate MIDI device

Chapter 12

Syncing ACID with Other Programs

ACID is a very powerful music composition tool all by itself, but it also interfaces well with other tools you may want to use. You can link ACID to other programs, using ReWire, MIDI timecode (MTC), or MIDI clock. ACID 4 can act as a ReWire mixer (host), while ACID 5 adds the ability to act as a ReWire device (client). This greatly extends your options for using ACID with other applications.

Using ACID as a ReWire Mixer (Host)

When ACID is used as a ReWire mixer, the ReWire client device is used just like any other Soft Synth in ACID. For this example we will use Propeller-head's Reason, but any ReWire client device will work in a similar manner.

To connect a client application to ACID:

1. Select Insert>Soft Synth from the main menu.

2. In the Soft Synth Chooser dialog box, click the ReWire Devices tab.

3. Select the ReWire device and channel you want to slave to ACID from the list of devices. For this example, select Reason Mix L/Mix R.

4. Click the Open ReWire Device Application button to start the ReWire application (Reason).

5. Switch to your ReWire device application and load instruments or the project you want ReWire into ACID.

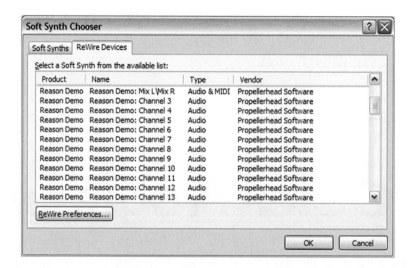

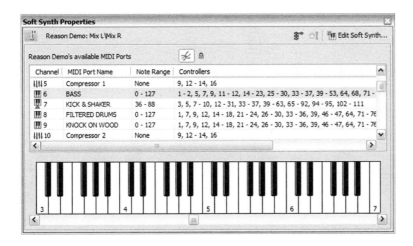

The Properties dialog box in ACID should now display any audio or MIDI instruments that are available in the ReWire application. The ReWire device will behave just like any other Soft Synth. When you press Play, the ReWire application will start playing. It sends its audio through the soft synth bus. You can control this bus just like any other bus, adjusting the volume or adding FX.

If the ReWire device supports MIDI data, you can assign this device to a MIDI track and play any instruments in the ReWire device that are exposed. This is particularly useful with programs like Reason that have a rack of instruments exposed individually.

Using ACID as a ReWire Device (Client)

ACID 5.0 has the ability to be used as a ReWire device in another application. For this to work properly, you must open the host application first before opening ACID. In the example we use SONAR as the master (host) application.

To use ACID as ReWire device in SONAR:

1. Open SONAR.

2. From the Insert menu select ReWire Device.

3. Choose ACID Pro 5.0 from the submenu. SONAR will insert ACID as a DXi soft synth and start the ACID application. Depending on your DXi Synth Options, you will have one or more tracks inserted into SONAR.

4. Open the project you want to use in ACID. The tempo of the project will be ignored, and SONAR's tempo will be used.

5. Return to SONAR and work as usual.

The SONAR transport controls will now start and stop ACID. Your ACID project

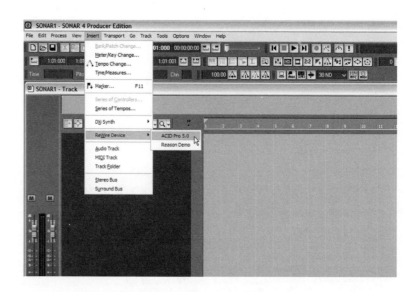

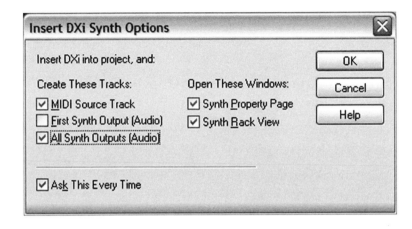

will be set to the same tempo as your SONAR project, and it should follow the tempo information and playback in sync.

Most ReWire host applications will allow you to control the number of outputs that are used. You can control how may outputs that SONAR uses in the DXi Synth Options dialog:

1. In SONAR, select View>Synth Rack.

2. In the Synth Rack, click the Insert DXi Synth Options [O] or press the letter O.

3. Select the output options for inserting DXi Synths. Check "Ask This Every Time" if you always want to be presented with this dialog box when inserting a DXi synth or ReWire device.

Selecting First Synth Output (Audio) will only expose ACID's Master L/R output. You must select All Synth Outputs (Audio) to see any additional outputs from ACID.

By default, ACID will expose the following ReWire outputs:

- Main Stereo (Master L/R)

- Rear Stereo (Rear L/R)

- Center/LFE pair

- One stereo bus (Stereo Port A)

- Two Mono buses (Mono Port 1 & 2)

You can configure ACID to expose up to 26 extra stereo buses and 32 mono ports when ReWired.

To configure ACID's ReWire outputs:

1. Connect ACID to SONAR.

2. In ACID, Select Options>Preferences from the main menu.

3. Click the Audio tab. The Audio Device type should be "ReWire Device Driver."

4. Click the Advanced button.

5. From the Advanced Audio Configuration dialog box, change the number of extra stereo ports (Max 26) or extra mono ports (Max 32) as desired.

6. Close ACID to exit the application.

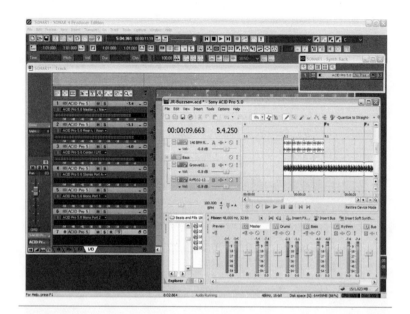

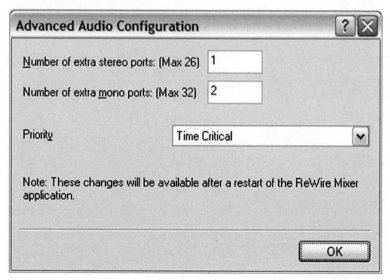

You must restart the ReWire device for the change to take effect.

7. In SONAR, close the ACID ReWire device and remove any tracks.

8. In SONAR, add ACID back as a ReWire device. The new outputs should be present.

You must restart the ReWire device in the host application for it to see these changes. If you see only two outputs, make sure you have all Synth Outputs (Audio) checked in SONAR's DXi Synth Options.

If you notice that ACID is sending only audio to SONAR through the first stereo output (Master L/R), it's because you haven't assigned anything to the other outputs in ACID. To use the extra outputs in SONAR, you need to route your ACID output to them using buses:

1. In ACID, select Insert>Bus from the main menu to insert a new bus.

2. Use the Playback Device Selector button on the bus to select the Re-Wire output you would like this bus routed to.

3. Use the Device Selection button on the track header to route a track to the new bus.

You should now have audio on the track in SONAR that corresponds to the bus output in ACID.

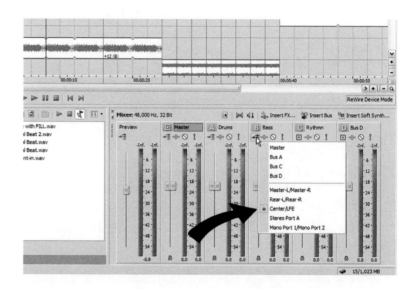

Syncing to MIDI Timecode

It is preferable to sync applications using ReWire, but sometimes you need to sync with an application that is not ReWire-enabled or is physically on another PC. You have two other options: syncing to MIDI timecode (MTC) and syncing to MIDI clock. In order to sync to MIDI timecode or clock you must have a MIDI output device available on your PC. This does not have to be a physical MIDI device. There are several software devices that will emulate a real MIDI device for the purpose of syncing two applications, such as the Sonic Foundry MIDI Router or MIDI Yoke. You can find these for free on the Internet. MIDI Yoke sets up eight virtual MIDI ports that you can route MIDI data just as if they were physical MIDI ports on your computer.

ACID works best as the master device when synchronizing to MIDI timecode. This is because it needs to be in control of the tempo changes.

To sync ACID to SONAR using MIDI timecode:

1. In ACID, select Options>Preferences from the main menu.

2. Click the MIDI tab.

3. In the top list box for MIDI output, check the MIDI device you want to transmit MTC on. In this example I have selected MIDI Yoke NT: 1.

4. Click Apply.

5. Click the Sync tab.

6. Under "Generate MIDI Timecode settings: Output device" select the same MIDI output you just enabled on the MIDI tab. In this example select MIDI Yoke NT: 1.

7. Select the frame rate you want to use. You must select the same frame rate in the slave application. Leave it "SMPTE Non-Drop 30 (30fps)" for now.

8. Click OK.

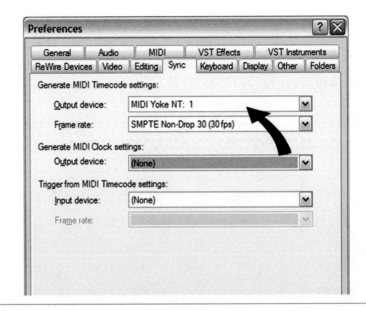

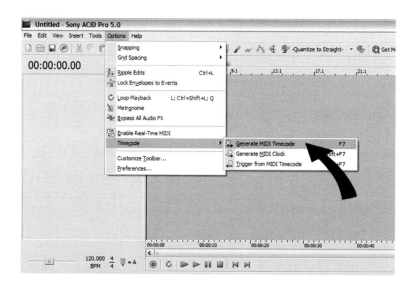

Now that ACID is set up to send MTC to the correct MIDI port, we have to tell ACID that we want to generate MIDI timecode now. Select Options>Timecode>Generate MIDI Timecode (F7).

ACID is now set up to generate MIDI timecode on the MIDI port specified. To complete the connection, we must tell the slave application to listen for MIDI timecode on the same port. We will use SONAR as the slave application, but any program that can sync to MIDI timecode can be used including external hardware sequencers.

To set up SONAR to receive MIDI timecode:

1. In SONAR select Options>Project from the main menu.

2. Click on the Clock tab.

3. Select SMPTE/MTC.

4. Under Timecode Format, select the format that matches the Frame Rate you selected in ACID. For this example use 30 FPS ndf.

5. Click OK.

6. Select Options>Global.

7. Click on the Timecode tab.

8. Select "Maintain current clock source and wait for timecode." This will keep SONAR listening for ACID to send MTC when you press Play in SONAR.

9. Click OK.

10. Select Options>MIDI Devices.

11. Choose the same MIDI input device as the output device you selected in ACID to send MTC. In this example we selected MIDI Yoke NT: 1.

12. Click OK.

You can now sync ACID and SONAR to MTC by clicking the Play button in SONAR and then switching to ACID and clicking the Play button. If SONAR doesn't respond, make sure you have Generate MIDI Timecode (F7) turned on in ACID.

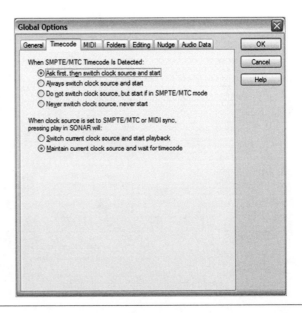

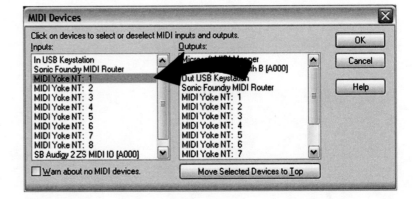

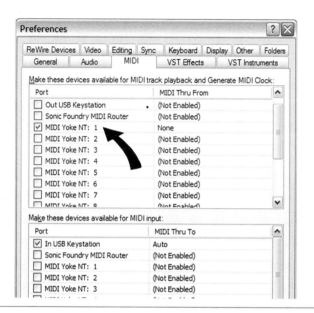

Syncing to MIDI Clock

Syncing to MIDI clock is a similar procedure as syncing to MIDI timecode. Unlike MIDI timecode, MIDI clock is continuous stream of ticks from the beginning of the project with no tempo change information. We will use SONAR in this example, but any application that can receive MIDI clock should work in a similar fashion.

To sync ACID to SONAR using MIDI clock:

1. In ACID select Options>Preferences from the main menu.

2. Click the MIDI tab.

3. In the top list box for MIDI output, check the MIDI device you want to send MIDI clock on. In the example select MIDI Yoke NT: 1.

4. Click Apply.

5. Click the Sync tab.

6. Under "Generate MIDI Clock settings," select the same MIDI input device you just enabled on the MIDI tab. In this case I selected MIDI Yoke NT: 1.

7. Click OK.

Now that ACID is set up to send MIDI clock to the correct MIDI port, we have to tell ACID that we want to generate MIDI clock. Select Options>Timecode> Generate MIDI Clock (Shift+F7).

ACID is now set up to generate MIDI clock on the MIDI port specified. To complete the connection, we must tell the slave application to listen for MIDI clock on the same port. We will use SONAR as the slave application, but any program that can sync to MIDI clock can be used, including external hardware sequencers.

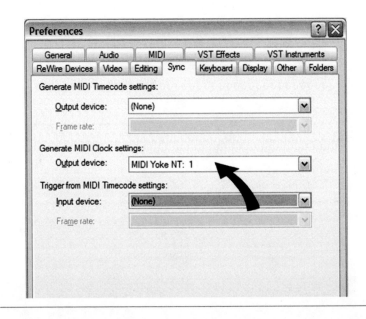

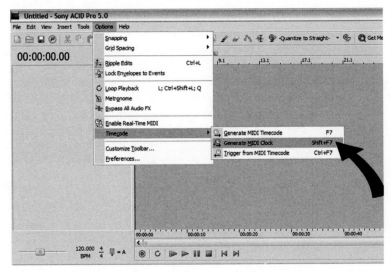

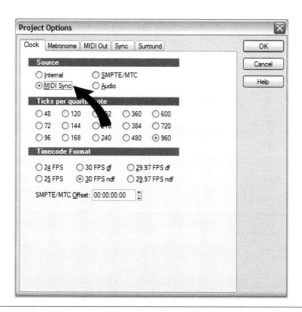

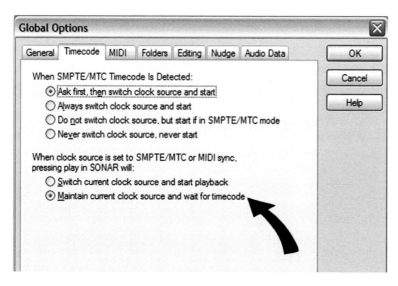

To set up SONAR to receive MIDI clock:

1. In SONAR select Options>Project from the main menu.

2. Click on the Clock tab.

3. Select MIDI Sync.

4. Click OK.

5. Select Options>Global from the main menu.

6. Click on the Timecode tab.

7. Select "Maintain current clock source and wait for timecode." This will keep SONAR listening for ACID to send MIDI clock when you press Play in SONAR.

8. Click OK.

9. Select Options>MIDI Devices.

10. Choose the same MIDI input device as the output device you selected in ACID to send MIDI clock. In this example we select MIDI Yoke NT: 1.

MIDI clock does not send tempo. It is up to you to manually adjust your slave application tempo to match the ACID project tempo (or vise versa).

11. Click OK.

You can now synchronize ACID and SONAR to MIDI clock by clicking the Play button in SONAR and then switching to ACID and clicking the Play button. If SONAR doesn't respond, make sure you have Generate MIDI Clock (Shift+F7) turned on in ACID.

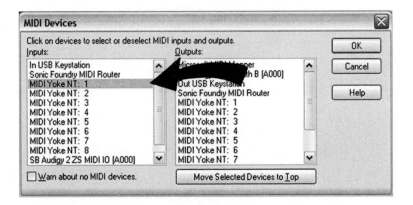

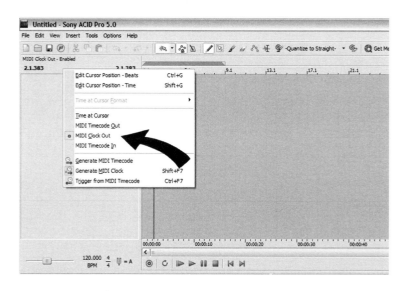

View Outgoing Timecode or Clock

It is often very useful to be able to view the outgoing timecode or clock in ACID's time display readout. This helps debug synch problems, because the time readout will tell you when timecode or clock is enabled or disabled.

To display the outgoing MIDI timecode or MIDI clock:

1. Right-click the ACID Time Display.

2. Select MIDI Timecode Out or MIDI Clock Out from the Context menu.

The Time Display will now show the outgoing MIDI timecode or MIDI clock. It will also display the fact that MTC or Clock is enabled or disabled.

Chapter 13

Applying Effects Plug-Ins

ACID comes with a rich selection of DirectX plug-in effects. ACID Pro 5.0 also supports VST effects and tempo-based effects. You can add effects to tracks, buses, or soft synths—which are just like buses. They can be inserted into tracks or routed to sends that can be combined with the mix.

DirectX Effects

ACID Pro comes with 18 DirectX Plug-in Effects from Sony's XFX 1, XFX 2, and XFX 3 series of plug-ins.

These include: Chorus, Multi-Tap Delay, Pitch Shift, Reverb, Simple Delay/Echo, Time Compress/Expand, Graphic Dynamics, Graphic EQ, Multi-Band Dynamics, Noise Gate, Paragraphic EQ, Parametric EQ, Amplitude Modulation, Distortion, Flange/Wah-Wah, Gapper/Snipper, Smooth/Enhance, and Vibrato. These DirectX plug-ins work with Sound Forge and Vegas as well, and any plug-in chains that you create with them can be shared among these other Sony applications.

Effects can be applied to tracks, buses, and soft synths, since a soft synth is just a special type of bus. You can follow the instructions on how to insert effects on buses for soft synths as well. Anywhere you see a reference to Bus FX you can substitute Synth FX. ACID Pro allows a maximum of 32 effects chained together on a single track or bus.

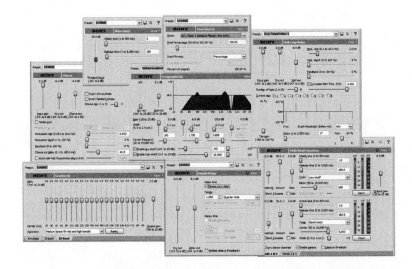

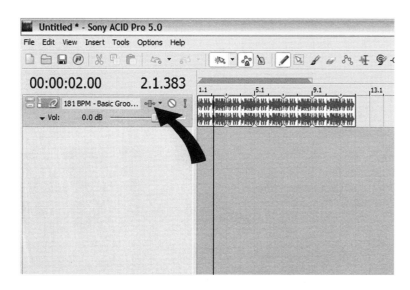

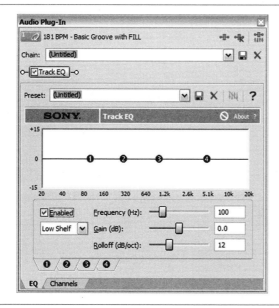

To insert an effect on a track, bus or soft synth in ACID:

1. Click the Track FX button on the track or the Bus FX button on the bus on which you want to insert an effect. Note: You can only insert FX on audio tracks, not MIDI tracks. For MIDI tracks, insert the FX on the Soft Synth bus.

2. If there is already a default effect on the track or bus, you will see the Audio Plug-In dialog box for that effect. If this is the case, click the Edit Chain button. This will bring up the Plug-In Chooser dialog. If no effect was present, the Plug-In Chooser dialog will launch directly from clicking the Track FX or Bus FX button.

3. From the Plug-In Chooser, select the plug-in that you want to add to the track or bus. The tree view on the left side of the Plug-In Chooser will filter the plug-ins by various attributes. The All view shows all plug-ins.

ACID Pro 5.0 supports VST plug-ins. These can be singled out by selecting the VST folder from the left Audio FX tree view in the Plug-In Chooser.

4. Click the Add button to add the FX (or you can also just double-click the plug-in name). Multiple effects can be added in a chain by continuing to select them and clicking the Add button.

5. Click OK when you have finished adding effects.

You can select an FX preset and adjust the parameters of each effect.

Effects Chains

Effects can be chained together with the output of one feeding the input of the next. These chains can contain up to 32 effects. You can also rearrange the order of the effects in a chain by clicking on the effect name and dragging them left or right across the chain.

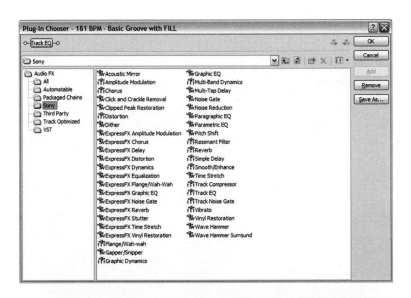

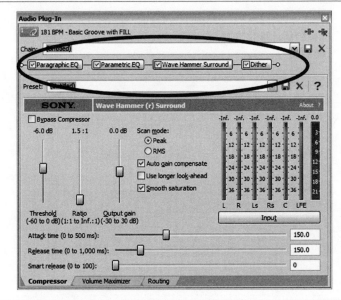

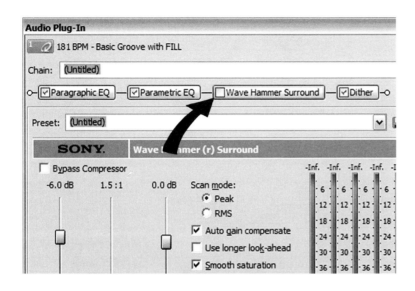

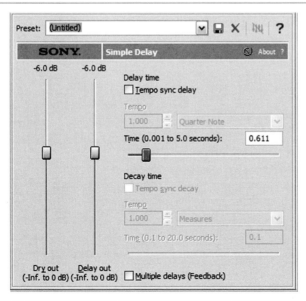

Each effect name in the chain has a checkbox next to it. This determines if the effect is active in the chain. You can quickly listen to how an effect is altering the sound by unchecking this box to disable it, and then checking it again to enable it.

You can adjust the order of the FX in the chain by dragging them left or right.

Tempo-Based DirectX Effects

ACID Pro 5.0 includes tempo-based DirectX effects. These include Amplitude Modulation, Flange/Wah-Wah, Chorus, and Simple Delay.

Tempo-based effects enable you to make effects that cycle, such as echoes and chorus, repeat on musical tempo boundaries without having to calculate the actual timing manually—which changes as the tempo changes.

In the example, we have the Simple Delay effect shown first in normal mode and then in tempo sync mode. When "Tempo sync delay" is un-checked, you must specify the delay time in thousandths of a second. If the project time signature is 4/4 time, and the tempo is set to 120bpm, that means there are two beats per second (120bpm divided by 60 seconds) or one beat every half-second. If you want the delay to be a half-beat behind, you must set the time slider to 0.25 (half of 0.5, which represents one beat). Try it and see.

Now check the "Tempo sync delay" checkbox. Notice that the time slider is grayed out and you have the ability to specify the delay amount as a multiple of the tempo (we will leave it at 1.0 for now) and note duration. Since we are in 4/4 time, a quarter note gets one beat. To have the delay be a half-beat behind, we set the delay to an eighth note.

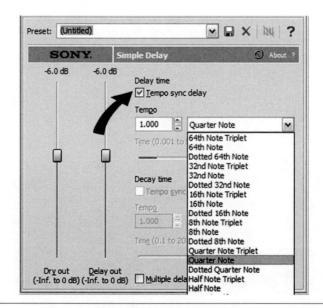

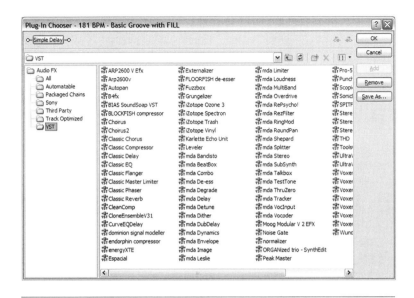

Not only is using tempo sync delay easier to set because there is no math involved—just set it to the musical duration you want—tempo sync delay is relative. That means if the songs tempo changes, the delay will remain an eight note (or half-beat behind), just as you wanted. In normal mode, the delay would drift out of sync as the tempo changes because it is fixed at 0.25 seconds which is only an eight note at 120bpm.

VST Effects Support

ACID Pro 5.0 supports VST effects. These effects can be used anywhere DirectX effects can be used, expanding your pallet of possible effects that work with ACID. There are no special instructions for adding VST effects. Just follow the instructions earlier in this chapter on inserting DirectX effects, except select the VST tab in the Audio FX tree view on the left side of the Plug-In Chooser.

Effects as an Insert or Send (Assignable FX)

If you are familiar with hardware consoles or other audio applications that mimic them, you are probably familiar with the terms Insert and Send. In ACID, an Insert is called a Track FX, and a Send is called an Assignable FX.

You should think carefully about whether to add an effect as an insert, as a send, or on a bus. If the same effect setting will be used for multiple tracks, you might consider using a send or bus instead to cut down on CPU utilization and make changing the parameters of the effect easier to manage, because you will have only one place to change them instead of on each track.

General rules to follow:

- Use Track FX to adjust things on a track that are unique to the track such as EQ, amp distortions, and filters.

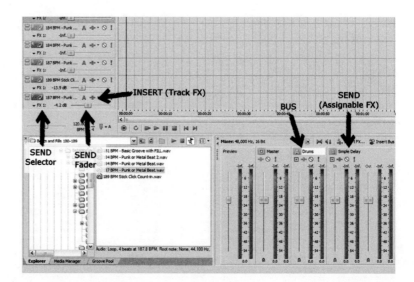

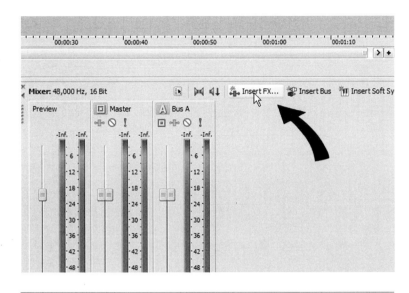

- Use Bus FX to adjust things at the output stage of the bus, such as limiting, compression, and Wave Hammering.

- Use Assignable FX to provide a common FX to multiple tracks, such as reverbs and choruses.

To create a send in ACID, use an Assignable FX. This will allow you to route multiple tracks to an effect chain while maintaining the ability to separately set the effects send level for each track. You can also set the send to be pre-fader or post-fader in relation to the volume of the track.

To insert an Assignable FX (Send):

1. From the Insert menu, select Assignable FX or click the Insert FX button over the bus area.

2. From the Plug-In Chooser, select up to 32 effects that you want to insert, clicking the Add button after each.

3. Click OK.

4. Adjust the FX parameters of each effect you added. You can switch to the various FX dialogs by clicking on their name in the chain.

5. Click OK when complete.

An effect send will be added to the bus area. You will notice it has two faders instead of one. These are individual input and output faders on the send.

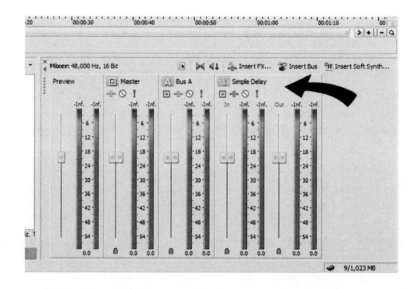

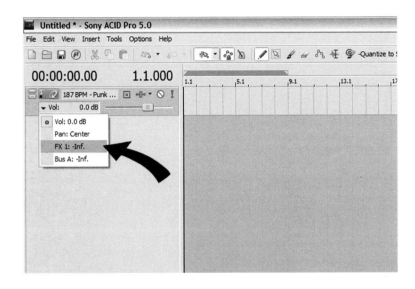

To send a track to an Assignable FX:

1. Go to the Track header and Click on the Vol: label on the left of the volume fader, and it will drop down a menu of assignments you can make for that fader.

2. Select the assignable FX you just inserted. The FXs are numbered 1 through 24. It should be labeled "FX 1:" if it is the first assignable effect.

3. Optionally, select Pre Volume or Post Volume for the send. Post volume is the default.

4. Adjust the fader for the amount of the tracks signal you want to send to the FX .

Using Assignable FX also allows you to independently control the wet and dry signal by setting the FX to 100 percent wet. Because the Assignable FX is on a Bus by itself, it can be panned separately in the stereo or surround space. This allows you to separate the effect from the source in a stereo mix.

Chapter 14

Mixing

Learning how to mix requires hands-on training and listening to different mixes and why they sound the way they do. If you are trying to achieve a certain sound, listen to other songs that have that sound. Try to dissect them and understand why they sound the way they do. When you think you have achieved the sound, place your song on a CD or tape between two of the songs you are trying to emulate and listen to the three songs in order. Did yours stand out as sounding different, or did it blend in? This is a good indication of whether you have achieved the sound you are looking for.

Approaching the Mix

If you haven't read chapter 8 yet, you should do it now. Approaching a mix has a lot to do with being organized and in control. ACID has tracks, track FX (inserts), assignable FX (sends), and buses, just like a hardware mixing console. The goal of the mix is make sure that all of the intricacies you put into your music are heard. No instrument should overpower the others (unless, of course, that is your objective).

It is a good practice to have buses set up for common instrument groups. Start by muting all of your buses. Then unmute the percussion bus if you have one. It helps if you group the percussion tracks into buses. This will allow you to control the volume of many tracks in the overall mix with one slider. In the example we will mix a pop song that has four buses: percussion, bass, rhythm, and lead. Each of these buses represents a section of the band that requires different equalization, compression, pan, and volume.

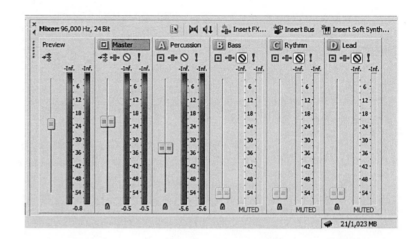

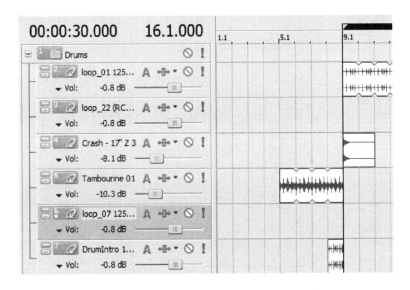

By using buses, you can divide the task of mixing into sub mixes. First, mix all the tracks that are routed to a bus from the faders in the track headers so that they are balanced. Start with the percussion and get them mixed. Then you move on to the next bus, muting the previous bus and unmuting this one, and mix those tracks so the instruments are balanced with each other. Move through each bus this way. Buses are helpful even on single instruments because ACID cannot have more than one loop on a track. You may have many bass tracks just to make up the one bass part in your song, and routing them all to one bus helps keep them all balanced with each other.

When you have submixed all the tracks into buses, you can use the buses to balance the submixes into the overall song. Start by bringing all the fades down except the percussion. Next, mix in the bass so that the drums and bass are balanced. Then move on to the guitars, and so on. Quite often, you will need to go back to the track faders and readjust a submix because it's just not fitting right with the rest of the song. You might even decide to pull a track out of a bus because it needs special attenuation of some kind. Using this technique, you should have an organized approach to your mix.

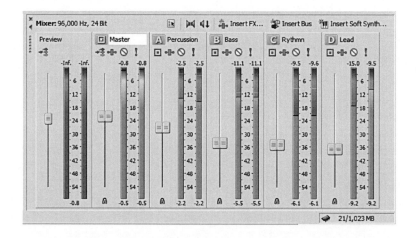

Inserts and Sends

Inserting a track effect or routing tracks to sends is covered in Chapter 13, Applying Effects and Plug-Ins. Now is the time to do an audit and think about whether you placed the same effect on multiple tracks that you might want to consolidate into a send or apply to a common bus. This cuts down on CPU utilization and makes changing parameters of the effect easier to manage, as you will only have one place to change them instead of on each track.

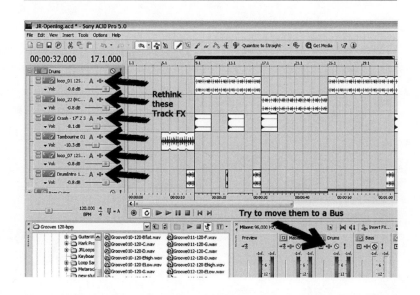

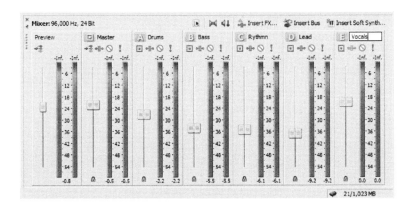

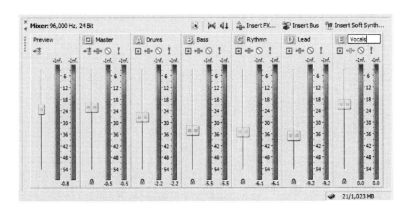

An Assignable FX (Send) works best in a wet-only setup. It is best not to let the FX do any mixing between wet and dry processed sounds. Use the ACID mixer to produce the dry portion and use the return aspect of the Assignable FX to sweeten the mix.

Buses

Buses allow you to control a collection of tracks while maintaining the relative volume between the tracks. Buses are a great organizational technique for grouping all the drums in a project under a single fader. You can add FX chains to buses just as you can with tracks. This also makes buses an ideal place to put common, FX-like compression or limiting, that multiple tracks will be using. The difference between a bus and a send is that a send splits the sound, routing it to both the track's bus and to the send at the same time. This allows you to control the amount of sound that is routed to the send. With a bus, all of the output is routed to the bus input.

To insert a bus:

- From the Insert menu, select Bus or click the Insert Bus button above the bus area.

A new bus will appear in the bus area. In addition to the master bus, you can have up to 26 buses labeled A thru Z. Buses can be physically assigned to external hardware or they can just be assigned to the master bus (by default).

To route a track to a bus:

- From the track header, click the bus assignment button and select the bus letter to route the track to.

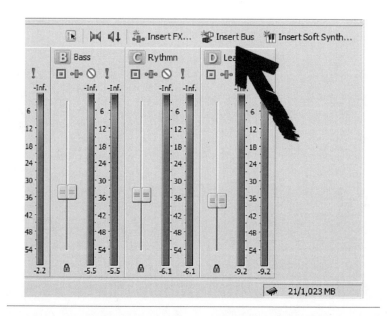

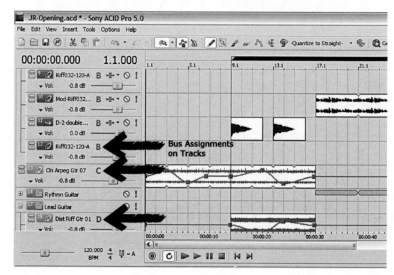

Bus Assignments on Tracks

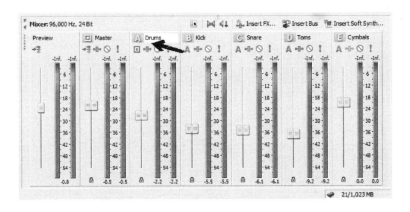

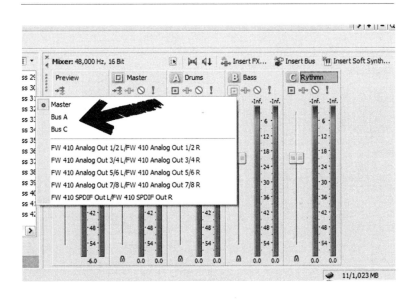

Bus-to-Bus Routing

By default, all buses in ACID are assigned to the master bus. ACID Pro 5.0 has the ability to route a bus to another bus. This second level of subgrouping allows even finer-grained grouping control. For example, if you have drum tracks made from one-shots, you probably have several cymbal tracks, several tom-tom tracks, or such. With bus-to-bus routing, you could route all the cymbals to a bus, all the tom-toms to another bus, and then route those two buses to another bus that is grouping all the percussion. In this way you can control subgroups at several levels.

To route a bus to another bus:

- Click the bus assignment button on one bus and change it from the master bus (the default) to another bus.

Automation

Buses can be automated with envelopes just like tracks. You can insert Volume, Pan, and FX Automation envelopes.

To view the bus cracks on the Timeline:

- In the View menu, select View Bus Tracks (B) or press the B key.

- Pressing the B key again will hide the bus tracks.

To insert an automation envelope on a bus:

1. Turn the bus track view on (use the B key).

2. Right-click on the bus track and select Insert/Remove Envelope.

3. You can select either Volume or Pan by default. If the bus also has FX on it, the FX Automation Envelopes will be available.

4. If you have an effect on the bus that you want to automate, select FX Automation Envelopes.

5. From the FX Automation Chooser

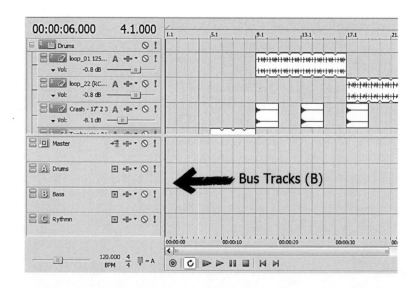

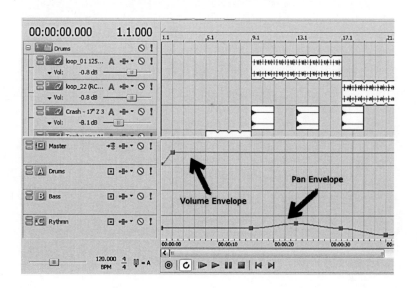

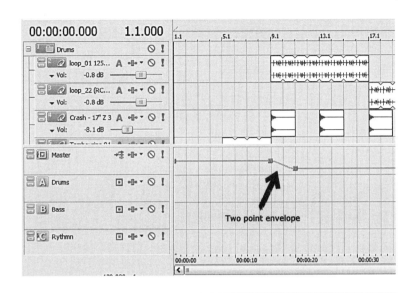

Two point envelope

dialog, check the parameters in the effect that you want to automate.

6. Click OK.

The envelope will be displayed on the track as a straight line. To modify it, you must add points to the envelope. There are two ways to add points to an envelope. You can manually add points or in the case of an effect, you can dynamically add points by directly manipulating the FX parameters that the envelope represents.

To add points to an envelope manually:

1. Double-click the envelope at the point in time you want to change to start, and a point will appear.

2. Double-click the envelope at the point in time you want to change to end, and a second point will appear.

3. Move this second point vertically to the new value.

As you have seen, it takes two points to affect a change. The first is the anchor point that establishes the start of the change. The second is the actual value that you want the envelope to change. You can see how easy it is to automate a change in volume, pan, or FX parameter over time. Even if you want a change to happen immediately, you still need two points.

If you want to temporarily change a parameter and then change it back, you will need four points. This is useful when you want to duck music under a vocal track. Follow the same procedure as with two points, but add two more to mark the length of the change and when to return to the original value. Then just pull down on the line segment between the two inner points to evenly modify both the second and third point values at the same time.

Sometimes it is easier to modify the envelope using the FX fader than entering parameters directly.

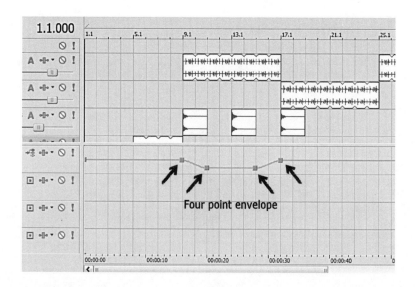

Four point envelope

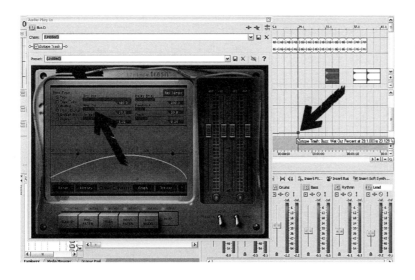

To add points dynamically:

Note that this works only for FX, not Volume or Pan.

1. Place the cursor at the place on the Timeline where you want to change the envelope value.

2. Open the effect and modify the parameter that the automation envelope represents. A point will be automatically be added to the envelope, and it will move up and down, changing the envelope as you adjust the fader in the FX plug-in.

You can also keep the plug-in FX open and move the point on the envelope up and down. The fader in the plug-in will move in relation to the point position on the Timeline, just like a real motorized automated console fader would.

5.1 Surround Mix

To do surround mixing you have to set your project up for Surround Sound.

1. Select File>Properties or press Alt+Enter.

2. Click on the Audio tab.

3. Change the Master bus mode to 5.1 Surround.

4. Optionally check "Enable low-pass filter on LFE." This will apply a low-pass filter on any track that is assigned to the Low Frequency Enclosure (LFE). You can also change the cutoff frequency here.

5. Click OK.

The Master bus will change from just one set of stereo faders to two sets of stereo faders (Front L/R, Rear L/R) and two mono faders (Center and LFE). You can control the master 5.1 surround mix from these four faders.

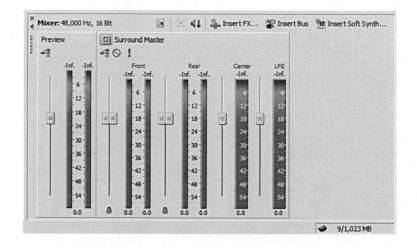

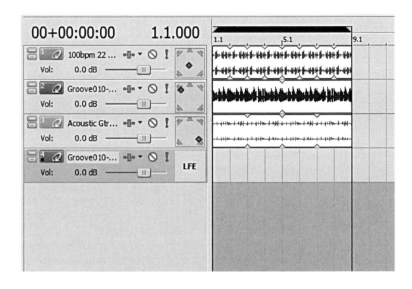

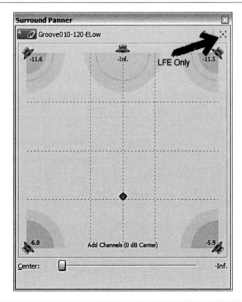

Notice that each track now has a surround panner. This allows you to assign the track to anywhere in the surround field by moving the red diamond in the middle of the speaker symbols. Double-click on the small panner to bring up a bigger one in a floating window.

You can route a track to the Low Frequency Enclosure (LFE) channel by:

1. Double-click on the surround panner on the track header

2. Click the LFE Only button.

The track will now be assigned to the LFE and only the letters LFE show in the surround panner.

If you want to monitor the mix in 5.1 and have a soundcard that supports six discrete outputs with 5.1 speakers attached, you can adjust the settings in the audio preferences to route the mix to these outputs.

To route audio to 5.1 monitors:

1. Select Options>Preferences.

2. Click on the Audio tab.

3. Select an audio device type that is 5.1-capable.

4. Select the stereo output pairs for front playback, rear playback, center and LFE playback.

When you move the surround panner on a track or bus, you should now hear the sound coming out of the respective speakers.

You can now mix using 5.1 surround just as you would a stereo mix (only with six master outputs instead of two).

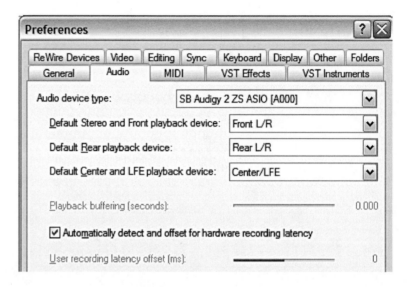

Chapter 15

Mastering

In general, mastering is the process of preparing a final mix for manufacturing. It is the last chance to add that final sheen to polish the sound. Typically, it is done on a stereo mixdown file and not a multi-track mix. At the mastering stage you add overall equalization, compression or other sonic enhancements to smooth out the sound. If the target media is CD, mastering ends with a final dither and resample to 16-bit/44.1kHz (CD sampling rate).

Many Sony users, including the authors, like to perform their final mastering in Sound Forge, but you can follow the steps in this chapter in ACID by rendering your final mix to a stereo file and then bringing it back into a new ACID project for mastering. Just add any of the effects covered in this chapter to the master bus in ACID.

Before you begin mastering, it is important to have a good monitoring system that you can trust. It also helps to have a dead room to monitor in. While building a monitoring room is beyond the scope of this book, it is important that you can trust what you are hearing coming out of your monitors. Use sound-absorbing material in your room with varying angles to absorb room echo and reflect standing waves.

It is also important to listen to your mix at an appropriate volume. If your monitors are too low you will tend to add too much bass to compensate for it. Crank up those speakers. Also test your recording in other environments. Take it out to the car, over to your friend's house, on your home stereo, against other commercial CDs, and so on. Listen to how it sounds and judge what needs to be changed. Then note how it must sound in your monitor room in order to sound good on other equipment.

Mastering Effects

If you are using Sound Forge to master, add each of these effects to the file one at a time. If you are mastering in ACID, these effects should be added to the master bus as a chain. Some common effects used in mastering are EQs, de-essers if there are vocals, compressors, and spatial frequency enhancers (in that order).

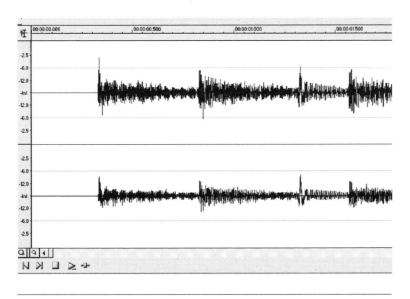

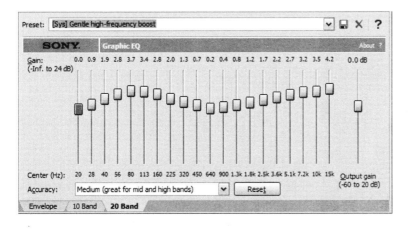

Before adding any mastering effects, trim your recording to the proper length. Remove any count-in or leader that you don't want to be heard at the beginning of the song. Do the same for the tail to eliminate dead space after the song ends, but be careful not to cut off any reverb tails abruptly. You might want to add one-third or one-half of a second of silence at the head and tail of the song just to pad the ends.

While each track probably has some kind of EQ, now is the time to balance the equalization of the whole mix. You want the mix to be rich with all frequencies but not have any one be overbearing. Lower the frequencies that are too loud and boost those that may be too low. If there are vocals in the song, you can use a de-esser to remove any unwanted sibilants or plosives.

After equalization and de-essing, compression is the next effect to apply. If you have Sony Sound Forge or Sony Vegas 5, you can use Wave Hammer or Wave Hammer Surround. If not, you can use the Track Compressor in ACID or purchase one of many finishing tools like iZotope Ozone 3, which will be covered later in this chapter.

To insert Wave Hammer on the master bus:

1. Click the Master FX button on the master bus. This will bring up the Plug-In Chooser dialog box.

2. Select Sony from the tree view on the left. This will filter out any effects that are not from Sony.

3. Select Wave Hammer from the list of plug-ins.

4. Click Add to add it to the plug-in chain.

5. Click OK to close the dialog box and open the Wave Hammer properties.

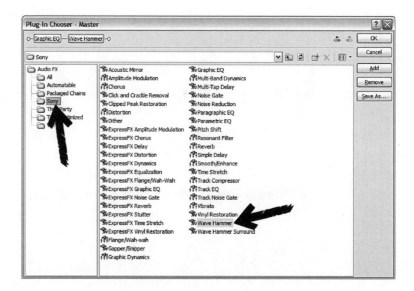

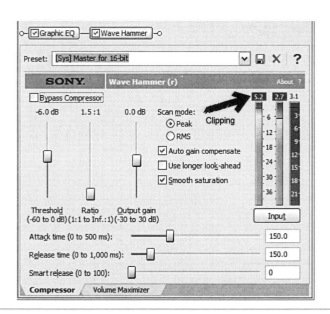

Wave Hammer is a compressor and a volume maximizer. From the Compressor panel, select the preset "[Sys] Master for 16 bit." This is always a good place to start for mastering, as it places a soft 1.5:1 compression to start with. Notice that there is a button under the VU meters to select input or output monitoring. Play your song all the way through and make sure there is no clipping on input (the red square above the VU meters). If there is clipping, lower your track volume levels until the clipping is gone. If there is clipping on output, you might want uncheck "Auto gain compensate" and lower the output gain until the clipping is gone. You don't want to feed clipped audio from the compressor into the volume maximizer stage.

Click on the red clipping indicators above the VU meters to reset them.

On the Volume Maximizer panel, you want to achieve maximum volume without clipping

1. Adjust the output level to the output you desire. I like to make it –0.3dB.

2. Adjust the threshold to set the level at which the dynamics processor kicks in.

If there is any clipping, adjust the output level to compensate. If you hear the compressor pumping, use a longer release time to compensate. A long release time will also preserve natural-sounding decays.

There are a variety of third-party tools that can be used in mastering. iZotope's Ozone 3 is a suite of mastering tools that I like to use. There is a downloadable demo version from the iZotope web site at www.izotope.com/products/audio/ozone/ if you want to follow along with this book.

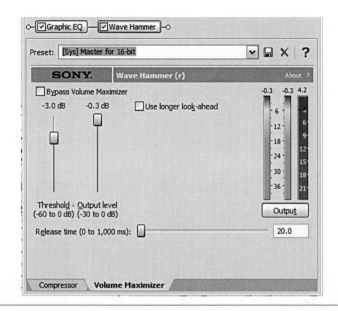

To insert iZotope Ozone 3 on the master bus:

1. Click the Master FX button on the Master Bus. This will bring up the Plug-In Chooser dialog box.

2. Select Third Party from the tree view on the left. This will filter out any effects that are not from third parties.

3. Select iZotope Ozone 3 from the list of plug-ins. If you installed both the DirectX and VST version, select the DirectX one.

4. Click Add to add it to the plug-in chain.

5. Click OK.

I like to start with the iZotope Ozone 3 presets. For mastering I like the "4 Band Mastering with Excitation and Widening" preset, which really gives a sizzle to cymbals, or the "Rock Master 4 Band With Excitation, Eq and Widening" preset for when I really want some punch. It is important to audition several presets to find the one that enhances your music in the way that you want.

To audition the presets in iZotope Ozone:

1. Set a looped portion of your song to play

2. In the iZotope Ozone properties dialog, click the Presets button.

3. Select each preset and listen to how it sounds until you find one that is pleasing to you.

4. Click OK (the green button on Ozone interface) to close the presets in Ozone.

5. Optionally, change any of the parameters in Ozone to customize the sound.

6. Click OK to close the Properties dialog box.

There are six finishing effects built into iZotope Ozone. It has a Paragraphics Equalizer, Mastering Reverb, Loudness Maximizer, Multiband Harmonic Exciter, Multiband Dynamics, and Multiband Stereo Imaging. iZotope Ozone can also be used as a Track FX or Bus FX to enhance drums, guitars, vocals, etc. It is a "Swiss Army Knife" type of tool.

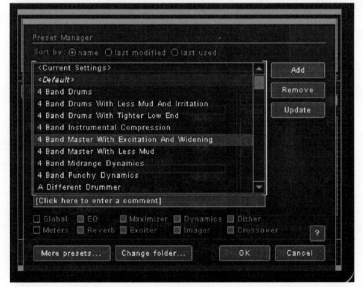

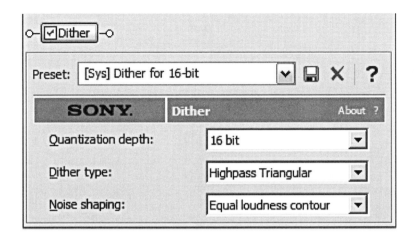

If you are mastering for CD you must get your file compliant with the 16-bit/44.1kHz audio that CDs require. If your file is already 16-bit/44.1kHz, then there is nothing you need to do but if you are working at 24-bit/48 kHz or 24 bit/96kHz you must use dithering and resampling to get the audio in a format a CD can accept.

To dither bit depth to 16-bit:

1. Add the Sony Dither to the master bus.

2. Select the preset "[Sys] Dither for 16-bit."

3. Close the Dither dialog in ACID (click OK if in Sound Forge).

Sound Forge has an option to resample your audio. If you only have ACID you must use Render As and pick "44,100Hz, 16-Bit, Stereo, PCM" as the template.

To resample your audio to 44.1kHz in Sound Forge:

1. From the Sound Forge main menu, select Process>Resample to bring up the Resample dialog box.

2. Select "[Sys] Resample to 44,100Hz with anti-alias filter" from the Presets.

3. Click OK.

Your audio should now be ready to be burned to CD.

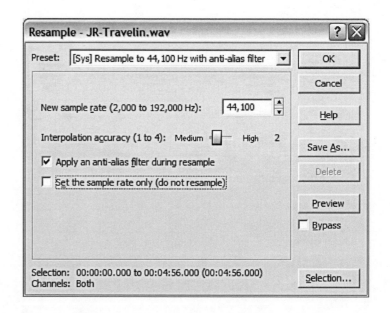

Chapter 16

Burning the Final Project

Once you have completed your composition, you can burn it to CD from within ACID. ACID Pro 5.0 gives you two options for burning your project on CD. You can fill up a CD one track at a time; this is known as track-at-once (TAO) burning. You may also burn your project as single CD image with multiple tracks. This is known as disc-at-once (DAO) burning. If you have a version of ACID before 5.0 you can only perform track-at-once burning. This chapter explains the difference between the two and how to create CDs using both methods.

The recordable CD media used in these examples can be:

- A blank CD-R disc (700MB/80min)

- A CD-R from a previous burn that has space on it but has not been closed

- A CD-RW disc that is either blank or can be erased

- A CD-RW that has more space on it but has not been closed

Note: Some audio CD players will not play CD-RW media. Use CD-R discs for the widest compatibility with stand-alone audio CD players.

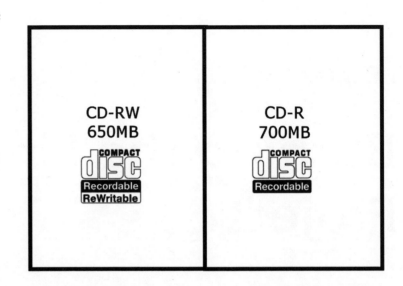

Track-at-Once CD Burning

Track-at-once burning was the only option available in versions of ACID before ACID Pro 5.0. It allows you to place one song at a time on the CD. It will automatically place the standard two-second gap between each song. You can continue to add songs to the CD as long as there is available space. When the CD is full, or you are finished adding tracks, you can close the CD so that it can be played in a tradi-

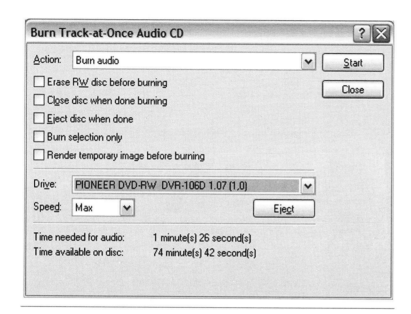

tional audio CD player. The advantage of track-at-once burning is that each song can be in a separate project, and the CD can be created over multiple sessions, perhaps spanning multiple days or weeks.

To burn a CD using the track-at-once method:

1. Load the project that you want to burn to CD

2. Load recordable CD media into your CD-RW drive

3. Select Tools>Burn Track-at-Once Audio CD.

4. In the Action drop-down menu select "Burn audio."

5. In the Drive drop-down menu select your CD-RW drive.

6. Click Start to start burning.

There are several options in the Action drop-down menu that are worth mentioning:

- **Burn audio:** Burns your project to CD. It is the option you will be using the most.

- **Test, then burn audio:** Performs a test burn where data is transferred to the CD burner just like a regular burn but no data is actually added to the CD, that is, the laser remains off. It's good for testing new CD burners or media. It tests that your computer can keep up with your CD burner without wasting media with failed burns. If the test burn is successful, the real burn is performed. This option takes twice as long because it performs the burn twice, once in test mode and once in real mode.

- **Test only:** Performs the burn test but does not burn.

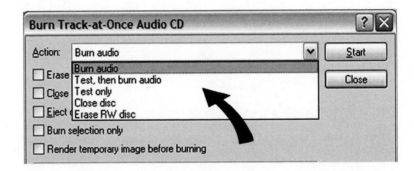

- **Close disc:** Makes the disc ready for playback on audio CD players. Until you close the disc, the disc can be read only by computer CD-ROM drives. This option is useful if you forget to check "Close disc when done burning" for your last track or if you decide not to add more tracks to a CD and want to close it. In other CD burning software, this may be referred to as finalizing the disc.

- **Erase RW disc:** Erases a CD-RW disc, useful when you just need to erase a rewritable disc but don't want to burn anything new to it. Otherwise checking "Erase RW disc before burning" has the same effect when burning.

The options on the Track-at-Once menu do the following:

- **Erase RW disc before burning:** Erases anything that is already on a RW disc.

- **Close disc when done burning:** Closes the disc. It should only be used when you have no more files to burn to the disc. This must be done so that the CD is playable in audio CD players, but once it is done, no further songs can be added to the CD.

- **Eject disc when done:** Ejects the disc from the computer. It is just a convenience operation. It does force the PC to purge its cache of what files are on the CD, so I like to leave it checked.

- **Burn selection only:** Burns only the selection, useful when you have more than one track in a project. It allows you to make a Timeline selection and burn it as a track. Then you can come back and make another selection and burn that as a track, and so on.

Action: Burn audio

☐ Erase RW disc before burning
☐ Close disc when done burning
☐ Eject disc when done
☐ Burn selection only
☐ Render temporary image before burning

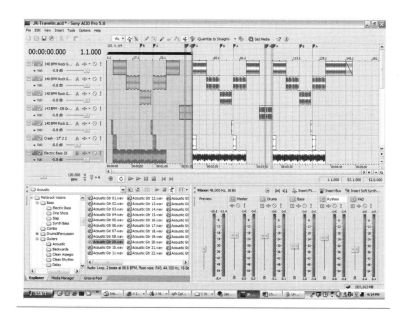

- **Render temporary image before burning:** Renders the project to your hard drive first and then burns the image as fast as your hard drive and CD burner can work together. It should be used if your computer cannot play your ACID project back fast enough to keep up with the CD writer. This might happen if you have a lot of effects or a lot of tracks in your project. If you are experiencing buffer underruns when burning, use this option to fix it.

Disc-at-Once CD Burning

ACID Pro 5.0 allows disc-at-once burning. You can burn an entire disc with multiple tracks in one session. This has an advantage over track-at-once burning because you have total control over the track gap. If you want to have two tracks that blend into one another, you must use disc-at-once burning. Until version 5.0, ACID was not capable of creating a CD with run-on tracks.

ACID Pro 5.0 introduces a new marker, the CD track marker. This tells ACID where each CD track begins. It is up to you to leave a gap between the tracks if you want two seconds of silence between song selections.

To insert a CD track marker:

1. Position the Timeline cursor at the point where you want to mark a new CD track.

2. Choose Insert>CD Track Marker or press the N key (for new CD track).

Once you have your tracks marked, save your project. You are now ready to burn in disc-at-once mode.

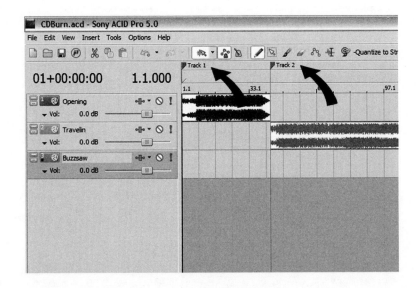

To burn a CD using the disc-at-once method:

1. Load the project you want to burn into ACID if it isn't loaded already. Make sure it has CD track markers, or else the disc-at-once menu option will be disabled.

2. Load recordable CD media into your CD-RW drive.

3. Select Tools>Burn Disc-at-Once Audio CD.

4. In the Drive drop-down list, select your CD-RW drive.

5. Select "Buffer underrun protection" if its available on your burner.

6. Click Burn CD under Burn mode.

7. Optionally, check "Render temporary image before burning" if you experience buffer underruns.

8. Click OK to start burning.

There are options in this dialog box to test before you burn just as in the track-at-once dialog. These are usually only selected when testing a new CD burner. You can optionally select "Automatically erase rewritable discs" if you have a previously used CD-RW that you want to burn. Finally, the "Eject when done" option is a convenience that lets you know when the disc is finished from across the room.

Chapter 17

Useful Formulas and Musical Aids

When dealing with ACID and other applications such as Sound Forge, you'll probably find it handy to know some basic, useful formulas and aids that will help you if you're constructing loops of your own.

Not many users know that a four-beat sample that's exactly two seconds long will loop perfectly in a tempo of 120bpm. Why is that? It's all in the math.

Calculating Tempo and Seconds

To find out the tempo a four-beat sample would best fit into:

Example: 240 ÷ 2 seconds = 120bpm

Similarly, you can find out the number of seconds you need for a four-beat sample to fit within a particular tempo. This especially comes in handy when using Sound Forge:

Example: 240 ÷ 80bpm = 3 seconds

If you have a sample that's two measures long in common time (making it a total of eight beats), just halve the number of beats or length of the sample to use the formulas above. If you have a three-beat sample, there are formulas for that too.

240 / (number of seconds) = (BPM)

240 / (BPM) = (number of seconds)

To calculate the tempo for a three-beat sample:

180 ÷ (length of sample in seconds) = (tempo the sample will fit into)

To calculate the length in seconds of a three-beat sample:

180 ÷ (tempo) = (number of seconds needed for sample)

If you noticed a pattern here, give yourself a cookie. As I mentioned before, it's all in the math.

The assumption that each second contains the number of beats per measure for 60 seconds (1 minute) gives us the numerical value you see at the beginning of the formula. You can compose formulas for other samples containing any number of beats using this method.

Calculating Delay and Decay

Though ACID Pro 5 has tempo-based DirectX effects like the Simple Delay plug-in, there may be times when you want to get your hands dirty and do it yourself, especially when constructing loops in audio editors such as Sound Forge.

To calculate delay:

$(60,000 \div 100\text{bpm}) \times 1$ (quarter note) = 600 milliseconds (or .6 seconds)

$(60,000 \div 120\text{bpm}) \times .5$ (eighth note) = 250 milliseconds (or .25 seconds)

$60,000 \div 100\text{bpm} = 600$ milliseconds (or .6 seconds)

$60,000 \div 140\text{bpm} = 429$ milliseconds (.429, or about .43 seconds)

60,000 / (BPM) x (note value) = (delay in ms)

60,000 / (BPM) = (echo or decay in ms)

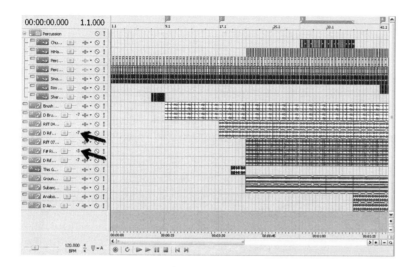

For the examples above, if you want the decay to last longer, multiply the result by how many beats you want the decay to last. For example:

(60,000 ÷ 140bpm) × (four beats) = 1,716 milliseconds (or about 1.72 seconds)

Transposition Line

ACID can pitch-shift loop events and tracks in increments of semitones, but ACID will tell you only the key you're pitch-shifting to on the event level. If you pitch-shift at the track level, ACID will tell you how many semitones you're shifting from the original key but will give you no indication as to what key you're shifting to.

In these cases, the transposition line will help you gauge precisely what key you're shifting to so that your track or tracks stay harmonious with the rest of your project.

If you're familiar with music theory, you'll notice that these intervals can form chords. For example, C (root), E (major 3rd) and G (perfect 5th) form a C Major chord.

To use the transposition line:

1. Determine your ACID project's key. Locate the key on the line. The example here assumes the key is in C.

2. Count how many steps from the project's key to the desired key you want to pitch-shift to. In this example, I want to pitch-shift a track to G, so I count seven spaces to the right to transpose seven semitones up, or five spaces to the left to transpose five semitones down.

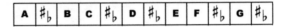

When you reach the end of the line, start from the opposite end of the line and continue. For example, if you reach the end of the line while counting left, start at the opposite end and continue left.

Typical harmonious intervals from a specific root note are:

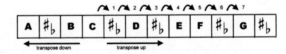

- Four semitones above (major third above root)

- Seven semitones above (perfect fifth above root)

- Eight semitones below (inverted third below root)

I	IV	V	I
F	B♭	C	F
C	F	G	C
G	C	D	G
D	G	A	D
A	D	E	A
E	A	B	E
B	E	F♯	B

- Five semitones below (inverted fifth below root)

- 12 semitones above (octave above root)

- 12 semitones below (octave below root)

Remember that these are only guidelines. You don't have to go a perfect fifth above, for example. You can simply detune a track instead of harmonizing, or go a semitone above or below for a dissonant effect.

If you're familiar with music theory, you'll notice that these intervals can form chords. For example, C (root), E (major 3rd) and G (perfect 5th) form a C Major chord.

Since ACID uses sharps rather than flats, use the equivalent sharp for a particular flat. For example, B flat equals A sharp.

I-IV-V-I Progression Chart

The most commonly used chords in music composition are the I chord, the IV chord, and the V chord. The combined notes of these three chords make up all the notes of the major scale. That means you can harmonize with any melody that uses a major scale with these three chords. For those unfamiliar with music theory in general, at left is a chart of common chord progressions that will help you with finding out what key contains which I-IV-V-I progressions.

From these three chords (I-IV-V) you can create the popular progression known as the 12-bar blues (a bar is a measure). There are many variations on the basic 12-bar blues pattern that closely follow:

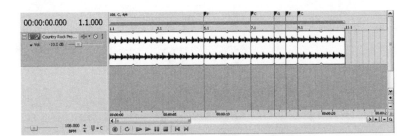

- Four bars of the I chord

- Two bars of the IV chord

- Two bars of the I chord

- One bar of the V chord

- One bar of the IV chord

- One bars of the I chord

One variation is to stay on the V chord for two bars instead of going to the IV chord for a bar.

As always, since we're dealing with music theory, this is only a guideline. The I-IV-V-I progression is the most common, especially in music genres such as popular music, but there are other progressions as well.

Ballads from the 1950s like *In the Heat of the Night*, *Tears on My Pillow* and thousands of others follow the pattern I-VI-IV-V. In this progression, the chords change every two beats (or half measure). This four-chord progression is only two measures in length. Another interesting ballad progression is the I-VI-II-V.

Many jazz songs use the II-V-I progression. There are also minor progressions like the VI-IV-I-V. Pop songs use progressions like the I-IV-I-V progression or the I-V-VI-V progression. You can see that these progressions are just variations on a theme. Use them as a staring point for making key changes in your music to capture the style you want to emulate.

Chapter 18

Final Thoughts

Since its introduction in 1998, ACID has continued to break new ground in loop-based music composition. ACID Pro 5 continues to innovate with its groove mapping, media management, and track folders. It continues to gives its users the features they have requested, like full ReWire support, improved MIDI, VST instruments, VST effects support, reverse playback, and more. Now that ACID can be used as a ReWire device, it can truly be integrated into whatever suite of tools you use on your digital audio workstation.

Continue to play with the software, consult the users guide and online help, visit the forums on Sony's site, and visit Digital Media Networks to learn even more about the various features and functions.

Above all, think outside-the-box—or more appropriately outside the loop.

Don't forget to chop up your loops:

- Slice 'em

- Dice 'em

- Pitch-shift 'em

- Time-stretch 'em

- Reverse 'em

- Flip them front to back

- Compose your own loops out of one-shots

- Record your own loops from scratch

- Put your unique signature on your music

ACID gives you the tools, and the authors of this book hope that Instant ACID has given you the foundation to take your music to the next level. Don't forget to experiment and have fun.

 TRAINING

VASST is Video, Audio, Surround, and Streaming Training. Here at VASST we help you master your preferred topic faster than you ever expected with immediate, accessible and thorough information. We offer a variety of training materials for different learning styles.

Whether you are looking for a book, a DVD, or an on-site trainer, VASST can provide tips, techniques, and solutions for all your media needs.

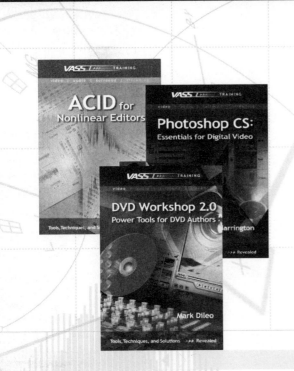

VASST Training Tours: visit vasst.com for current tour dates. We offer seminars on Cameras, Lighting, Editing, Surround Sound, and other general media topics. Training on specific applications by companies such as Adobe, Sony, Ulead, Pinnacle, AVID, Boris, and Apple is also available.

www.vasst.com

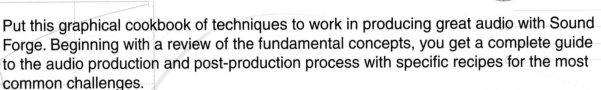

Instant Sound Forge®
Jeffrey P. Fisher

Put this graphical cookbook of techniques to work in producing great audio with Sound Forge. Beginning with a review of the fundamental concepts, you get a complete guide to the audio production and post-production process with specific recipes for the most common challenges.
Softcover, 209 pp, ISBN 1-57820-244-2, $24.95

Using Soundtrack: Produce Original Music for Video, DVD, and Multimedia
Douglas Spotted Eagle

Beginning with a review of essential audio concepts, you get a complete, illustrated orientation to Soundtrack's features with practical examples and tutorials. The companion CD includes tutorial materials, plug-ins and original loops worth $200.
Softcover with CD-ROM, 240 pp, ISBN 1-57820-229-9, $34.95

Instant Surround Sound
Jeffrey P. Fisher

Unravel the mysteries of multi-channel audio processing for musical and visual environments. This comprehensive resource teaches techniques for mixing and encoding for surround sound. It's packed with tips and tricks that help the reader to avoid common and not-so-common pitfalls.
Softcover, 224 pp, ISBN 1-57820-246-9, $24.95

Find CMP Books in your local bookstore.

www.cmpbooks.com